To: David + I

Simon   2024.

ATLANTIC ROWER

by

Simon Howes

UK Book Publishing.com

Copyright © Simon Howes, 2024

The moral right of this author has been asserted.

All rights reserved.

No part of this publication may be reproduced, stored in a retrieval system, or transmitted, in any form or by any means, without the prior permission in writing of the publisher, nor be otherwise circulated in any form of binding or cover other than that in which it is published and without a similar condition including this condition being imposed on the subsequent purchaser.

Editing, design, typesetting and publishing by UK Book Publishing

www.ukbookpublishing.com

ISBN: 978-1-917329-01-9

To Sara

"You can never cross the ocean unless you have the courage to lose sight of the shore."

Christopher Columbus

CONTENTS

ONE

Background

I WAS BORN in July 1955, into a family of seafarers. My father was a Rear Admiral, my great-grandfather a full Admiral and his father a Vice Admiral. Later in life, given my genealogical ancestry and my love of the sea, I was confident that rowing an ocean would be a piece of cake. How naïve was I…

I was brought up in the Wiltshire countryside and enjoyed a very happy childhood, but never had a chance to try my hand in a rowing boat. During school holidays, my first job had been working as an assistant to a team of surveyors, helping them build a railway bridge over the main road in the Wylye Valley. My job had been to hold the theodolite, in between playing vingt-et-un in the staff canteen. Everyone on the site spent most of the working day smoking Embassy Gold or Woodbines. More time was taken up playing cards and smoking with the senior surveyors than concentrating on the job in hand. When the moment came to crane the roof into position onto the newly built abutments, it immediately became clear that someone had screwed up. It didn't fit! I never worked on a building site again.

I was never an academic and went out of my way not to read books. As a 17 year old studying for geography 'A' level, I was stunned to learn that the Specific Ocean was in fact called the Pacific Ocean. Hardly a good omen for my future transatlantic aspirations. I failed most of my exams including 'A' level Economics. Despite this I would eventually take up a career as a stockbroker.

As the second son, I was expected to make a career in the Royal Navy as soon as I left school. Too dim to consider either university or the Royal Navy, my exit strategy was to sign up as a jackeroo in Western Australia. In 1973 work prospects in the UK didn't look great, with half the country on strike and unemployment soaring. I headed to Australia and spent almost eight years there working on the stock exchange trading floor. In the 80s I returned to London before eventually settling in the South of France.

I have spent much of my life behaving irresponsibly. I had taken up smoking Benson & Hedges special filters at school and would only quit the habit when I was in my 50s. I calculated that if I lined up the number of cigarettes I had smoked, the distance would have been greater than that of a marathon. After quitting cigarettes, I discovered the joys of Montecristo No:2s and continued to drink copious quantities of Chateau Gloria.

On the morning of my 50th birthday, our eldest daughter suggested that I was spending too much time gardening. I said, 'Don't worry, darling, one day I'll do something to make you really proud of me.' When she suggested, 'What, like climb Mount Everest', I assured her I wouldn't be doing that anytime soon…

I have never been really fit and I had no intention of changing this regime, even after purchasing a rowing boat. I was the unlikeliest person in history to attempt to row an ocean.

TWO

The Lightbulb moment

In January 2020 just before the Covid pandemic, Sara and I went on holiday to Antigua. We had recently moved to the Isle of Wight and were in need of a little winter sun. Staying at The Inn, we were sipping cocktails on the beach overlooking the entrance to English Harbour. We witnessed a young man rowing into the bay alone to great fanfare. A couple on the beach told us that he had just rowed solo across the Atlantic Ocean, from La Gomera in the Canary Islands to Antigua. As a participant in the annual Talisker Whisky Atlantic Challenge, he had won the solo class in this sponsored event. This annual Challenge was becoming increasingly popular and for me this was the lightbulb moment. Throughout this book I refer to the TWAC as the Challenge.

I was so impressed by his win and the boat's obvious provenance and pedigree that I decided to try to buy her then and there. Almost as soon as he had stepped ashore, I approached him. He politely suggested that I might like to get in the queue as four other people had already expressed interest. I said, I'm not planning to be in a queue, I want to buy her immediately. He gave me his price and I shook his hand. All he had to do was arrange for shipping back to the boatyard in Essex in the South East of England. It was one of the easiest transactions in the history of transactions; no haggling or bartering. I recited to him a couple of verses dreamt up years earlier by a friend on the trading floor of the old Sydney Stock Exchange.

'Do the business while you can and you'll be a happy man. He who tries to do too well, will neither buy nor sell.'

This solo rower was a consummate sportsman. We had agreed a full price and the die was cast. I returned to the beach and mused that this was turning into one of those very expensive foreign holidays.

I would need to change the name of the boat and I needed a website if I was to support a charity with a Just Giving portal. Back in England I asked a web provider to check if anyone had used the name www.atlanticrower.com to my surprise the name was available. The boat would be christened *Atlantic Rower* and my website would be named after her as soon as possible.

The boat was delivered to me in Portsmouth docks on Friday 15th May 2020. I had no proper instructions, I knew nothing about rowing, let alone about how to row across an ocean. With trepidation I towed her back to the Isle of Wight on the car ferry. This wasn't a simple exercise: the car, trailer and boat together were in excess of 50 foot long. I soon discovered that the tailboard hit or scraped the ground every time I drove on or off the ferry. Had I passed a long-load-articulated-lorry driving test, this process might have been easier. Having never driven a low trailer before, it took me a further couple of hours to uncouple her! *Atlantic Rower* had arrived and was now parked in our drive.

The excitement really began when Sara and I emptied the contents of the boat into our garage. The feeling was similar to opening a party bag. So many new toys to play with and so little knowledge of what they all were. Exciting times as more and more voyeurs poked their heads through our front gates in complete disbelief.

A few days later reality finally dawned on me. I had made another impulsive purchase without even considering the ramifications. I had bought an **Ocean rowing boat**. Was I really planning to use her for the purpose for which she was built? Or would she end up with the disused exercise bike we had lurking in the back of our garage? Trouble was that she was 25 foot long and not so easy to hide.

I should mention here for those not familiar with this sport, an ocean rowing boat is not similar to the kind of rowing boat you might find on your average village pond. Originally made of plywood, then fibreglass and more recently using carbon fibre. *Atlantic Rower* was made of fibreglass and built by a boatyard in Essex in 2019.

They are designed and built for rowing very long distances in the open ocean and are fitted with all sorts of sophisticated equipment. These boats are now much safer than the original plywood boats constructed in the late 1960s. Today they are kitted out with a lot of modern safety equipment, although this doesn't always mean that these extras work properly. Anyone who has attempted to row an ocean over the past 60 years, will have discovered that things don't always go to plan. At least 14 people have died while ocean rowing and hundreds more have been rescued at sea, including myself…

To get a feel for how relatively new ocean rowing is, go back to 1969 when a young man named John Fairfax became the first solo in history to row across the Atlantic Ocean. His ocean rowing boat was called Britannia and was designed by Uffa Fox in Cowes. He set off from Gran Canaria, exactly the same island from which I was to depart in early 2023. He regularly flagged down other shipping, to shower, have a hot meal or restock his larder. After 180 days at sea, he arrived in Florida to a hero's welcome. Upon completion of his voyage, he received a telegram from the crew of Apollo 11, some of whom had walked on the moon a few days earlier.

An extract from this telegram reads: *'Your accomplishment was one of a resourceful individual, while ours depended upon the help of thousands of dedicated workers in the United States and all over the world. As fellow explorers, we salute you on this great occasion.'*

Signed: Neil Armstrong, Edwin (Buzz) Aldrin and Michael Collins.

By 2019, the Ocean Rowing Society International (keepers of all ocean rowing statistics), recorded that more than twice as many people had been into space, than had ever rowed the Atlantic Ocean solo and unassisted.

I reminded myself of the Australian slogan used by the Victorian state government back in 1975 *'Life be in it'*, encouraging people to be more active. So, I enrolled myself in several RYA maritime courses. I soon received numerous smart certificates for passing tests. This always surprised me as I had never been anywhere near top of a class in my life. The subjects included: first aid, sea survival, short-range radio, navigation and seamanship, amongst others. None of this seemed very relevant to rowing a boat, but these courses were compulsory if I wanted to enter the Challenge in 2021. By now I had the bit between my teeth and was determined to take up the Challenge. Mat helped me launch her in Wootton Creek. His father reminded me that this ocean rowing was really a sport for the young, suggesting I would be better served aboard an enormous gin palace! Launching an ocean rowing boat is a two man job. The rudder can only be attached once the boat is on a slipway or in the water. Unlike other craft the rudder is inserted from underneath the hull – simultaneously you need a second person to bolt it in place in the aft cabin. I soon learnt the intricacies of handling a 25-foot rowing boat, just through playing around in the creek outside our house.

To participate in the annual Challenge, I discovered that it was compulsory to fit out the boat with a huge amount of safety gear. All rowers were sent a long list of essential accessories. I checked the inventory which had come with *Atlantic Rower* and was pleased to discover that some of these items were included in my original purchase. I would need to update my ownership details, re-register with various authorities and change lots of batteries. I was thankful that a BGAN did not feature on the list for the 2021 Challenge event. A Broadband Global Area Network system enables rowers to send live pictures home from anywhere on earth. To operate this system, you point the box towards the sky and they act like an aerial, connecting to satellites. Easy to lose overboard and incredibly expensive to replace. I certainly had no desire or need to send out live recordings from the ocean.

Wading through this list, I noticed it was obligatory that all rowers should carry two fire extinguishers. I guessed these must be a requirement to extinguish cigars or cigarettes while rowing.

It was around this time that I discovered Amazon Prime. I had never done online shopping in my life. Almost everything on the vast accessory list could be purchased over the internet. Our postman couldn't believe his luck: he delivered truckloads of parcels to our house for weeks on end, keeping him and the Post Office in business. Talk about compulsive shopping, I was the man…

I also decided to bite the bullet and replace my 25 year old Nokia 3310 with an Apple iPhone. This was another life changing moment for me. I could now navigate in coastal waters, while watching stock prices and reading my emails at the same time.

By the middle of 2020 I had enrolled myself in the annual Challenge. I would be on the start line with 35 other boats in December 2021. Before this challenge I needed to train and get a bit fitter. My initial training was predominantly off the Isle of Wight, followed by a very short stint in the North Sea.

You will all realise that on a rowing boat you always look backwards, so it's very difficult to see what's in front of you. This probably explains why over the course of two summers training on the Solent, I managed to hit the yellow North cardinal off Cowes once, the green buoy opposite the Royal Yacht Squadron twice and the red buoy in Wootton Creek several times. My oars are still coated in yellow, green and red paint to this day. I enjoyed rowing over to Seaview, dodging the hovercraft and making it back to the marina in East Cowes. I regularly stopped for lunch in Osborne Bay, adjacent to Osborne House, and I spent a couple of nights sleeping aboard *Atlantic Rower* in Newtown Creek.

A requirement of the annual Challenge was that entrants have at least 24 hours of rowing experience in darkness. My first overnight experiment was on the Solent. In the middle of the night, I heard a voice shouting out through a megaphone: 'Simon, watch out behind you'. I turned to discover that I had drifted into the main shipping lane near Portsmouth. I was about to be run down and crushed by a huge car container ship. I rowed like stink to get out of the way and had a narrow escape. The skipper of the Southampton pilot boat saved my life that night. He was one of several friends without whom and without their sound advice, I would never have contemplated rowing an ocean.

I kept the boat in East Cowes marina, fortunately run by very understanding people. However, even their patience was eventually tested, as I continually crashed into other moored boats when returning from training sessions. After some months they suggested I move moorings in the marina, into one big enough to house the Queen Mary. This had a significant impact on my life. I no longer had to offer grovelling apologies to grumpy yacht owners every time I returned to the marina.

I resolved that I would never call out the RNLI nor the Coastguard. Both organisations save the lives of people in real jeopardy. *Not* solo ocean rowers. It's one thing to endanger one's own life doing something silly, but a completely different thing to endanger the lives of those in the emergency services. To cover myself at sea, I took out a rescue insurance policy with Sea Start. As the name suggests they operate in the same manner as the RAC for cars, but for boats in distress. This turned out to be one of the smartest decisions I ever made.

Late in the summer of 2020, as part of my training, I decided that I should circumnavigate the Isle of Wight before attempting the Atlantic. The island has very strong tidal movements and timing is critical. Around the Solent, a solo rower can't row against an incoming spring tide, due to the force of the water. I rowed out of East Cowes marina at dawn and headed towards The Needles. On this occasion I resolved not to stop for lunch at The Hut in Colwell Bay. I surprised myself by rounding the iconic Needles by early afternoon. Then rowed like I'd never rowed before down to St Catherine's Point, on the southernmost tip of the island. By twilight the swell was growing as was the wind from the South. I decided to pause for a rest and deployed my normal sea anchor, on about 70m of chain and rope in Watershoot Bay. I then settled in for a delicious dinner aboard *Atlantic Rower* with a good claret.

Everything was going fine until around 22.00 hrs, when I heard the loud sound of rotor blades nearby. I looked up from my cabin and hovering above the cliff was an enormous AW189 Coastguard helicopter. The noise from its five-bladed main rotor was deafening. I surmised that the appearance of a coastguard chopper so far from home base at this time of night, was unlikely to be a routine jolly. I felt in no danger despite the fact the seas were now pounding my little boat. Clearly, I hadn't called them, but somebody on the cliff top in front of me must have raised the alarm, thinking I was in imminent danger. Nothing was further from the truth. My dilemma now, was how to call them off. If I waved at them from the deck, they could have misread that signal to mean I needed help. Equally if I had tried to call them up on the radio, I would have never heard a word they were saying.

This wasn't an option given the mind boggling noise from the two General Electric CT7-2E1 turboshaft engines. I decided the best course of action was to shut the hatch door and finish dinner. After ten minutes they disappeared – leaving me disappointed that I hadn't been able to thank them personally.

For me, problems tend to come in threes. I had checked the tide timetable and figured that I should be able to lift anchor around 03.00 hrs and continue my circumnavigation. I snoozed for a couple of hours and was awoken by winds gusting at 35 knots from the south and a swell, the like of which I had never seen before. I decided that it was time for me to get out of there. Row for my life, so as not to be washed up on the rocks directly below the St Catherine's Point Lighthouse. I stood on the rowing deck, my strength sapped by the waves and the wind. I tried lifting the anchor – then realised that it was caught on something. I considered cutting the anchor rope to free myself, but by now the weather had become so inclement, I figured that my boat would be swept onto the rocks. If I tried this my survival chances would be slim at best. Thank the Lord for my Sea Start subscription! It's now 04.00 hrs, so I called the emergency number and a charming Dutchman answered the phone. He asked for my subscription number, which I couldn't find. He told me that he had an active subscription for my old rigid inflatable boat 'Don't Tell Mama', but couldn't see anything about a rowing boat in his records. I asked him to look again... After what seemed an eternity, he discovered that indeed *Atlantic Rower* was paid up and fully covered. This was one of those hallelujah moments for me. He agreed to jump out of bed and come out to help me, cut the anchor rope and if required tow me away from the rocks. This whole rescue was one fantastic service. Everyone with a boat should have a Sea Start subscription; he literally saved my bacon. After cutting the anchor rope and pulling me away from the rocks, he then tried with his powerful twin-engines to lift the sea anchor. It was stuck fast; after several attempts we had to let it go. Later that day I discovered that I had dropped anchor on top of a notorious shipwreck graveyard. After this escapade, I decided that a circumnavigation of the island was for the birds. Perhaps in a four-man rowing boat on a calm day it would be feasible, but I wouldn't recommend this to any other solo ocean rower.

My next training episode was supervised, somewhere just north of the River Crouch. I had never been to the North Sea, but I had this image of it being a cold, wet and miserable place. I wasn't disappointed, but I had never imagined that the sea would go out for miles and miles at low tide. Moses must have stretched out his hand on my first day. Just when I thought it was safe to go rowing, the waters *parted*, in my case *departed,* and I was left stranded for six hours on the mud. The boat was grounded and I felt like the world's greatest idiot… I settled into supper, opened another good bottle of claret and turned off my radio. I didn't want to be disturbed by the instruction crew, none of whom were very impressed. I felt it best not to request assistance; there would have been nothing they could have done to help.

I towed *Atlantic Rower* back to the Isle of Wight, knowing that I needed to enlist the services of an experienced ocean rower to teach me privately. Soon enough I found the ideal person. Having recently crossed the Atlantic, she had experience in all things rowing. The most important piece of advice that she gave me was in regard to fitness. 'How fit do I need to be to row an ocean?' I asked her. 'Simon, don't worry about that too much,' she replied. 'You'll become very fit as you row across the Atlantic!' Having spent most of my life eating, drinking and smoking to excess, this was music to my ears. I worked out that I could save myself a small fortune by not having to sign up one of those expensive personal trainers. I took her at her word and didn't sweat too much on my Concept 2 rowing machine in the garage.

My days' training became severely limited by the Covid-19 lockdowns; the government banned us all from having fun on the water. I spent time kidding myself and telling anyone who might listen, that I would try another circumnavigation of the island sometime soon. In the final event this never happened.

I would depart East Cowes marina early morning, in the hope of not being spotted by the Harbour master. I wanted to avoid the embarrassment of him or fellow boat owners witnessing me tangle with the chain ferry as I made my way out of Cowes harbour. I would row down the coast to Colwell Bay to arrive just in time for elevenses. Drop anchor and swim over to the best restaurant on the island. Then order a large Bloody Mary with a dozen fresh oysters (I am an oysterholic). After elevenses I always concluded that it would be much quicker to row back to East Cowes, rather than make another attempt at circumnavigation.

This fitness regime worked well for me. It reminded me of Lord Andrew Lindsay's larger than life approach in the film *Chariots of Fire*. The rank amateur: balancing glasses of champagne on the hurdles to perfect his technique. I would later play the theme tune from this movie again and again, to inspire me while rowing to St Lucia – stirring stuff. On the subject of hurdles, I was to discover later that you can overcome hurdles by thinking big and by turning a Challenge into an Adventure. There is an enormous difference between the two, especially if you wished to row an ocean.

In the summer of 2021, it dawned on me that the Challenge start was just a few months away. I still wasn't completely confident that I was ready to row an ocean. I called up Duncan at his renowned ocean rowing academy. Duncan is an inspiration. I learnt more about rowing a boat over four days training with him, than I had learnt in all the time since I had bought the boat. Few people in the ocean rowing world can be classified as completely professional – he is just that. In my opinion he is by far and away the best ocean rowing tutor. Armed with so much fresh knowledge, I spent as much time as possible practising all that he had taught me on the Solent. This involved many more pit stops at The Hut in Colwell Bay. While this type of training was certainly not something that Duncan would have sanctioned, by the end of that summer I felt I was ready to have a go on the Atlantic Ocean.

THREE

The 2021 Challenge (a rather short Chapter)

I had no idea what to expect when I arrived in La Gomera, a couple of weeks prior to the start of the 2021 Challenge.

Back in 2005, I had entered a pre-war motor car in a 1,000 mile, 24-hour race around the streets of Italy, called the Mille Miglia. The event in 2005 was being held to celebrate the 50th anniversary of the race win by Sir Stirling Moss and his navigator Denis Jenkinson. In 1955 they had completed the 992 mile drive at an average speed of 99mph. An exceptional achievement, especially as the bulk of the race is held on back roads. No motorways or anything like that either then or now. The selection committee estimated that there would be well over four million spectators for this race, making it the biggest live sporting event, anywhere on Earth at that time. Sir Stirling Moss was on the starting grid again for the 2005 Mille Miglia, in the same Mercedes 300SLR which he had driven 50 years earlier. The Mercedes-Benz Museum in Stuttgart had shipped his winning car down to Brescia in Italy for the race start. There was one big difference between that event and the upcoming 2021 Challenge. Despite the huge entry fee for a car and driver, the race sponsors of the Mille Miglia handed over gifts to every single driver. These Chopard watches, personalised mobile phones etc, were worth well in excess of the full entry fee, even before we started driving!

The Challenge committee did a great job for all the rowers. I am very grateful for that; it is a very well run event for everyone involved. By the end of November 2021, Covid-19 was becoming a serious threat to all global sporting events. So full credit must go to the Challenge staff, who ensured the annual race from La Gomera in the Canary Islands to Antigua would go ahead. We were ordered to wear face masks at all times to avoid any risk of contagion. I was truly amazed that nobody arrived into La Gomera, before the start, infected with Covid-19. For sure we did notice several Fred Olsen ferries, turning back to Tenerife before they had even unloaded any passengers. Clearly this was nothing to do with Covid!

I should also mention here, that a huge number of friends and other know-it-alls, were convinced that I was a complete disaster waiting to happen. In fairness to them, I was the only rower taking a taxi every morning from the hotel down to the marina, arguably too unfit to walk down the hill. I wasn't spotted sprinting along the beach before breakfast or at any other time for that matter. I certainly wasn't glued to one of the water rowing machines laid on for the rowers in the marina. I preferred to eat a full English breakfast while this nonsense was going on. Most afternoons, other rowers were spotted polishing their rollocks in the boat park. I was so confident of victory, that I was knocking back copious quantities of gin & tonic in the Blue Marlin bar.

On the subject of my fitness, Tom, a good friend from Fishbourne, had recently reminded me of what he had witnessed only two years earlier. He had been a marshal in September 2019, at the weekly Parkrun on the Isle of Wight. He couldn't believe his own eyes when he spotted me participating in this event. He knew better than most, just how unfit I was, and was completely staggered to see me jogging along. When I collapsed after just one lap, on the ground in front of him, asking for a stretcher to take me away, he just scratched his head. Six months later when

I told him I was planning to row the Atlantic Ocean solo, he looked at me in total disbelief. But Tom was one of only very few people who didn't try to talk me out of it. Clearly, he had enormous confidence in my ability.

While nobody wanted me to fail, I could sense that some people were incredulous that I had even entered the event. Other people were openly vocal, using phrases such as 'this foolhardy challenge'. It would be fair to say that very few people expected me ever to arrive in Antigua, while I was supremely confident that I would make it to the other side, alive and well.

The penultimate inspection of all of the boats resulted in my having to spend more money on items which I was confident I would never require. These inspections were serious stuff; nobody was going to be rowing anywhere, unless they passed them. In La Gomera, *Atlantic Rower* was one of the final boats to be inspected. The light was failing – it had taken me the best part of four hours to lay out all of my gear on the tarmac. I quickly removed the tins of canned spinach from my rations, fearing that the safety team might disqualify me before the start for impersonating Popeye. I would ensure that I was the quickest rower in the history of the Challenge to reload my boat. It took me a mere six minutes and ten seconds, breaking all previous records in the process. It also meant that once at sea I had absolutely no idea where I had put everything.

While in La Gomera, all rowers had to attend a very serious daily briefing at 09.00 hrs. This briefing was presented to us by the Challenge event safety committee. The start date was almost upon us; I knew many of the competitors well enough to want to crack a joke at one of these briefings. When asked at the end of the briefing 'Are there any more questions?', I was going to ask the question, in front of everyone. 'Will I be able to keep the silver trophy, when I win the event?' This would have caused a riot in the tent, so I decided to keep my mouth shut.

A few days before the start, I had rowed out beyond the entrance to the marina for a bit of last-minute training and a rather unpleasant 'Man overboard drill'. Accidents happen, but on the way out I had collided with a large stationary passenger ferry. Apologies to Fred Olsen, but I did more damage to my rowing boat than to the ferry! On the day before the start, I had been ordered by the event safety team, to get in a bit more practice. Sara recorded a video of this as she honed in on me and my boat. She commented that 'Simon was just trying to work out where the buoys were located outside the harbour wall. He didn't want to be seen hitting them all, in front of the world's media the following day. He had rowed out carefully so as not to hit the Fred Olsen ferry again. At the same time, he was looking at his safety harness, trying to work out how to put this on. Clearly, he hadn't worn this before'. On the morning of the race as we walked down to the quayside. Sara took a photo of a T-shirt worn by one of the super fit competitors, just in front of us. It stated on the back in bold letters **'You'll never row alone'**. As I was pointing this out with my finger, she commented in a very loud voice 'unless you're a madman!'

Sunday 12th December 2021 loomed. I was race-ready, after my last-minute tuition delivered by Duncan in the late autumn. I was also certain that I was the most unfit rower participating. I had enjoyed myself with Sara for the past fortnight in and around La Gomera. We had discovered a great little restaurant in the back streets of the town, with an excellent wine list. We had the opportunity to entertain a fellow solo rower with his Swiss family for dinner at this same restaurant. In return for a good dinner, he helped me with some final technical assistance just before the start. I still had little idea of how to insert the first set of coordinates into my chart plotter, as prescribed by the Challenge safety team. This was something technical which I had never really understood.

I just couldn't afford to do a repeat of my North Sea stunt and end up going the wrong way!

Many of the rowers spent hours daily polishing their hulls ahead of the start. Whereas we spent as much time as possible getting a tan beside the hotel swimming pool. We also had great fun in the Blue Marlin bar. Rowers tended to congregate there most evenings before the race start. The camaraderie between the rowing teams was infectious and the atmosphere was electric. I should mention here that ocean rowers in general are some of the most interesting people I've ever met. Many of them have climbed mountains, run marathons and trained as elite athletes. We made some really great friends ahead of the kick-off.

The only real difference between *Atlantic Rower* and the other 34 boats was that I had no corporate sponsorship. The lead sponsor of the Challenge at the time was a whisky producer, so other wine and drinks sponsors were not encouraged to participate. This meant that without sponsorship, I was only responsible to myself. If things didn't exactly go to plan, then it would be impossible for me to let any corporate sponsors down. It followed that I was never asked to give lectures and talks to corporate entities or be behoved to anyone. With the benefit of hindsight this turned out to be a good decision. Eighteen months earlier, I had made the decision not to take any of this rowing too seriously. I was determined to have fun and enjoy the moment, even if I finished last (which I eventually did).

December 12th 2021, the three other solo rowers and myself were the final four to depart from La Gomera. As other participants made last minute adjustments to their row boats and the starting gun was fired, I was spotted still eating Twiglets in my communications cabin. Embarrassingly, when the moment came for me to row out of the marina, I still had one rope attached to the dock. This caused much laughter and delayed my start. At two-minute intervals we made our way past a large

Spanish warship, which appeared to be firing indiscriminately into the air, adding to the mesmerising excitement of our departure. Departing from La Gomera rather reminded me of being at a football match. A lady whom I had never met before in my life, had been screaming at the top of her voice as I left the marina, Si------mon, Si------mon. I was grateful for any support that I could muster. On the quayside, I saw the owner of our favourite French restaurant, and she appeared to be in tears. We had cleaned her out of her best Bordeaux wines and I was now leaving town to do a spot of rowing. She too had grave reservations for my welfare, with very good reason.

I had some difficulty rowing in the narrow channel outside the marina, despite yesterday's practice – I kept crashing into those plastic marker buoys by mistake. I rowed past a chap on his Lilo and thought to myself, well if this is the Atlantic Ocean, what have I got to be worried about... I'd been expecting raging seas out here. Eventually (hours later), I lost sight of La Gomera and settled down for supper at sea.

I continued to row on through the night, determined to take line honours in the event! I was hoping that my experienced lady weather router, would tell me if I was rowing the wrong way, via text sometime the following morning. In the event this never happened. I had decided in the early hours of day two at sea, to switch over my autohelm with a spare. To explain: if your ocean rowing boat is fitted with a ST2000 autohelm, they tend to overheat after about four hours. Originally these units would have been designed and manufactured for yachts and boats moving on a relatively constant bearing. Solo ocean rowing boats tend to be thrown around more at sea by the prevailing sea state, causing the hydraulic arm component to work overtime. The movement in a four-man boat fitted with this system is less pronounced due to their higher speed through the water. The advice given to solo rowers was to have two or three spare units.

These should be changed over on a regular basis. To do this, you have to stop rowing, ship the oars and switch off the autohelm in the comms cabin. Then crawl into the back of the aft cabin and swap over the units... All of this while being clobbered by waves, breaking over the boat.

Having replaced my autohelm with a spare, I emerged from the hatch and stood upright on the rowing deck. At that critical moment and without my sea legs, *Atlantic Rower* was broadsided by a large wave. I slipped on the damp rowing deck and was thrown forward, landing on my right elbow. This was smashed into the steel component which secured the footrest. The pain was excruciating; I knew instantly that I had caused serious damage. However, I decided to wait for several hours to gauge if this was just a pulled ligament and not a cracked bone. During this time, I became aware of a presence on the port side of the boat. A pod of three killer whales (orcas) appeared nearby. They took very little notice of me, but gave me the opportunity to take pictures of them as they swam past. Just to get them on film lifted my mood, despite my disappointment.

Around 14.00 hrs, on 13th December 2021, I knew that I was in real trouble. Despite the searing pain I acknowledged that I couldn't even lift my port oar. I couldn't ever remember reading of anyone rowing an ocean with one arm and decided my time was up. I used my satellite phone to contact the Challenge safety officer and he agreed to send a rescue boat. I had only rowed 38 nautical miles so this was a very sad moment for me. I felt down but not out. I was eventually towed back into La Gomera with a full film crew aboard the rescue vessel, to ensure maximum embarrassment and good coverage of my disaster. I was very grateful for having been rescued. It was now around 22.00 hrs. I ensured my rescuers received bottles of the 2006 and 2007 Chateau Gloria vintages from my aft cabin, as a small thank you gift. The Challenge doctor was on hand and was very helpful.

We agreed that the best thing was for me to get back to the UK as soon as possible for proper treatment. Hospital facilities on the small island of La Gomera were very limited.

A Challenge official made it abundantly clear to me within minutes of my arrival back into the marina, that the next few years' events were already completely fully booked out. I translated this to mean, don't even think about doing this ever again! Rather than being disappointed, this was music to my ears. I could now plan my very own ocean adventure, without all the razzamatazz. I would also ensure that my rowing adventure would be of a greater distance than the Challenge. I would eventually try for St Lucia from Gran Canaria, an extra four or five days for a solo rower. I had learnt a lot from this very brief experience, met a lot of very interesting people and been very impressed by the planning for the whole Challenge event. I flew home the following day in the knowledge that I had survived and so had my boat. It certainly had been a Challenge for me and I had failed dismally, but I would live to fight another day.

FOUR

If at first you don't succeed, try and try again

I had a great Christmas at home with the whole family, something which I had never expected to be doing a fortnight earlier. My right arm was in a sling but my desire to have another go at the Atlantic was stronger than ever. The Challenge episode behind me, I was just counting the cost of this aborted attempt to row an ocean. Transporting row boats to and from La Gomera from the UK is a very expensive business. My boat was due to be shipped back to the boatyard in Essex, arriving sometime in March 2022. I decided to have my old ST2000 autohelm removed and replaced it with an EV100 system. This turned out to be a good idea. I also decided that I didn't wish to arrive in St Lucia with a sore bum. So I rented a state of the art rowing seat from a chap in Holland – this too turned out to be a great success. It caused no damage to the runner on the rowing deck and it would enable me to take the existing rowing seat along as a spare. This would be handy if the rented seat went overboard in a storm. I should explain that the rowing seat on these boats is not a fixed unit, it slides back and forth on eight wheels, similar to those you might find on roller skates.

I had promised Sara a proper holiday on my arrival in Antigua. After all, she had been through a lot more stress than I, especially during the build up to the Challenge. This had been followed by literally hundreds of *Atlantic Rower* supporters calling her, to check everything was alright after my accident. We were both exhausted and flew off to St Lucia in January 2022. While there on holiday I decided to call in to meet the CEO of the IGY Rodney Bay marina. I will never forget the day I met Sean. He runs one of the busiest marinas in the Caribbean. The annual ARC sailing race finishes in Rodney Bay and he had a lot more on his plate that day to think about, than my interruption. Our conversation went something like this:

'Sean, I've decided to row the Atlantic next year in a 25-foot row boat, when I'll be almost 68 years old. I've also decided to try to make land here in Rodney Bay. Do I need to worry about booking a mooring in advance? Also, can you offer me any advice on customs and immigration clearance after my arrival?'

Only one person in history had ever attempted to row solo and unassisted to St Lucia from Europe. This happened almost 26 years earlier in 1997, when an Englishman at the age of 39 had made the crossing in 116 days. He had been very lucky to survive, due to a shortage of food and water. You can only imagine what Sean must have been thinking as he sat there looking at me. Whatever he thought about the probability of this happening, he was simply fantastic from that moment on. Nothing would be a problem, but perhaps I could let him know when I thought I might be arriving in my row boat next year… We shook hands; he is now a friend for life.

We returned to England in February 2022 and I collected my boat. As previously mentioned, one of the scariest things with an ocean rowing boat, is trying to tow it behind a car. I had never been great at navigation at the best of times and on my return trip, I managed to get completely lost. You might think finding your way back onto the A3 from Essex would be relatively simple, but for me it was a complete nightmare. Somehow missing all the correct road signs, I ended up in the town of Petworth. It took me at least three or four circuits of the town to find my way out. After several minor trailer accidents, hours later and completely shattered, I arrived at Gunwharf Quays in Portsmouth. Then, it only remained for me to be told that I had missed my ferry, I would have to wait hours for another one. I knew from that moment on that rowing 3,300 miles across the Atlantic Ocean would be a darn sight easier, than towing my boat anywhere in the South of England.

I received a very kind invitation from the committee of the Challenge, to attend a black-tie dinner in London in May. This was to celebrate the successful arrival of all the Challenge rowers (bar one!), into English Harbour. I was abroad that weekend, so was unable to attend, but I was asked if I could do a short film clip to be aired during the celebrations, and I was only too happy to oblige. This was eventually released on a big screen for all the attendees that evening. A bit like the television programme, 'This is your life' compered by Eamonn Andrews. My message to all those attending went as follows:

'Hello everyone, it's Simon here. I've been asked to say a few words by the Challenge committee. I'd like to say well done to everybody, for getting to the other side. I watched every single one of you, actually rowing in on the live broadcast. You must all be very proud, so congratulations. For myself, I've just started rowing again in the last couple of days. Hopefully, I'll be back rowing properly later this year.' I carried on, 'As Yogi Berra said a long time ago: It ain't over till it's over; so watch this space and have a lovely evening, bye.' This was met with rapturous applause. I doubted very much that a single person at the dinner seriously believed I would ever try to row the Atlantic Ocean again… Only I knew at that time that about eight months later, I would be going it alone.

I returned to East Cowes marina for some final training during the summer of 2022. However, weather conditions conspired against me. There were only a few days when it was even possible to row out of the River Medina into the Solent. On one of those days, I had rowed over to the Needles. On my return late afternoon, I spotted the PS Waverley (the world's last sea-going passenger-carrying paddle steamer). As I rowed past Yarmouth, she was about to overtake me and came to within 50m of *Atlantic Rower*. Hundreds of tourists on the decks started to cheer at the top of their voices. They couldn't stop waving and clapping their hands. This carried on for several minutes; it was really very embarrassing – what did they know that I didn't know? As they steamed past *Atlantic Rower*, I mused that the skipper of the paddle steamer must have made an announcement on his Tannoy system. Explaining to his passengers that I was just returning to the Isle of Wight, having rowed the Atlantic from the USA. I felt as though I had just won the Vendée Globe Round the World yacht race, it was really very funny and I'm still laughing now!

It was also around this time, I decided to ask a knowledgeable local friend to spend a couple of hours aboard *Atlantic Rower* with me. I needed him to explain some very important technical issues which I had not yet mastered. I self-promoted him to the rank of 'Captain'. He had already sailed the Atlantic many times and his knowledge and teaching ability were both simply excellent. Without his help I would almost certainly have ended up being shipwrecked in the Azores. Up until this moment I was convinced that my row boat had an autopilot. I had no idea that an autopilot and an autohelm are two very different things. Remember, I had absolutely no experience of boats prior to buying *Atlantic Rower*. I was stunned when 'the Captain' explained to me that my rowing boat did **not** have an autopilot. I had always presumed that if I placed a waypoint on my chart plotter, then hit the 'Go To' button, I would arrive at my destination. So long as my course over the ground (COG) and my bearing to waypoint (BTW) were aligned on the deck repeaters, I would automatically arrive at the waypoint. All normal boats and yachts using chart plotters have the autohelm wired into the chart plotter, but not my rowing boat! This new information completely changed my life, literally and forever. I understood for the very first time, that the chart plotter on *Atlantic Rower* was just a map. After this startling revelation, 'the Captain' helped guide me through many other chart plotter features. By lunchtime that day, I felt confident that I could now row at least 3,300 statute miles to St Lucia, on my own.

A week later the boys in Cowes suggested that I should use the services of Will to antifoul my boat ahead of my next Atlantic attempt. I met him at the Medina boatyard and within 30 seconds he had given me a breathtaking sales pitch. After completion, I was to discover that dry shaving using the hull of *Atlantic Rower* as a mirror, was more effective than using the one in our bathroom at home! I didn't know then, but have subsequently discovered, the actual polisher was none other than Leanne. Barnacles on the hull of a boat cause friction and slow the boat down. I would still have to jump into water over three miles deep, twice during my crossing. This preparation of the hull made the removal of barnacles a darn sight easier, especially while being prodded by sharks.

The boat was fitted out with a Schenker water maker which was located in the communications cabin, hereafter referred to as the comms cabin. This cabin is located in-between the small sleeping cabin at the forward end of the boat and the rowing deck. It was wired up to a couple of new lithium batteries; these in turn were being charged by two Solbian Flex solar panels. The solar panels were located on the roof of the forward and stern cabins. On a sunny day, I knew I could comfortably produce 26 litres of drinking water in one hour. During the row I drank seven or eight litres of water daily. I stored excess fresh water in a couple of plastic jerry cans. This was perfect for general washing and cleaning the salt off the solar panels. Twice daily I cleaned the solar panels so they maintained their efficiency by charging the two lithium batteries even on overcast days.

Prior to the Challenge I had purchased a large number of Radix dehydrated meals direct from the company in New Zealand. In my opinion, this was better than the other expedition food available on the market at the time. Dehydrated food, mixed with fresh water and cooked on a Jet boil, was not half as good as the rare roast beef served up at Simpson's on the Strand. However, each meal contained about 800 calories so it kept me alive. I packed 170 of these meals, plus a further 85 ready to eat *wet meals*, to be used if my water maker blew up at sea. In addition to this, I packed 48 Snicker bars, 48 Mars bars, 48 Kit-Kats, several chocolate Grenades, Twiglets and lots of nuts. Altogether, this enabled me to consume approximately 5,000 calories daily throughout the voyage. I would still shed over 8kg of body weight during 72 days at sea. I packed all the food and snacks into the four deck hatches on the rowing deck. This would create great ballast if *Atlantic Rower* capsized.

The only safety items I would use when I started my own adventure a few months later, were: a VHF radio, a rented satellite telephone and a mobile Garmin GPS. When John Fairfax rowed the Atlantic in 1969, he wouldn't have had even half this kit and he had a real adventure.

By late summer 2022 my boat was packed up, ready for another delivery, in yet another container back to the Canary Islands. This time to Puerto Rico marina in Gran Canaria. Prior to shipping the boat back to the Canary Islands, I had to trailer her back up to the boatyard in Essex. This excursion was no easier than the last one from Essex to the Isle of Wight. I can now confidently state that 50-foot waves crashing onto a rowing deck are less scary than those potholes in the road between the Dartford crossing and Burnham-on-Crouch.

At this time, Sara and I had already decided that the fewer people who knew about my second attempt to row the Atlantic solo the better. Many people and many friends had already very kindly donated to the charity which I was supporting. I felt I had let a lot of people down after my aborted first attempt. Let's face it, if you have a bet on the Grand National and your horse falls at the first fence, it is very disappointing. Meanwhile back at HQ, we still had lots of excitement to look forward to. Our first granddaughter was to be christened soon, there were numerous parties happening and life was good with little pressure from anywhere. I was going to be able to enjoy Christmas 2022 with my wife and children at home. I could forget about my sequel until after New Year. Then I would be able to start my own adventure on a date to suit me, sometime in January 2023.

La Gomera race day 2021 © *Atlantic Campaigns/World's Toughest Row*

The rower being sprayed down just after the start of TWAC 2021.
Note the plastic marker buoys! © *Atlantic Campaigns/World's Toughest Row*

East Cowes Marina

Atlantic Rower rounding the iconic Needles. Photo courtesy of Ian Plested

Atlantic Rower in the Solent. Photo courtesy of Ian Plested.

Sea Survival course

The Titanic fenders, rope ladder and raw concrete wall in Puerto Rico Marina

FIVE

Puerto Rico marina, Gran Canaria

Tuesday 3rd January 2023. I had booked seat 1A on the EasyJet flight as I felt this could easily be my last flight anywhere! I landed at 18.40 hrs, in Gando Airport on the outskirts of Las Palmas, in a state of excitement. I jumped into a cab with two huge suitcases stuffed full with all my fragile boat accessories, which I hadn't been able to pack prior to shipping.

The cab arrived in the town of Puerto Rico an hour later, I had chatted to the taxi driver during this short ride about my row. By the time we arrived I could gauge that he felt I should be sectioned under the mental health act. It was dark when I arrived in this sleepy seaside town. I booked into a reasonably cheap hotel behind the marina, called Hotel IG Atlantic, a fitting name I thought. This was a great base for the next two weeks, while I made final preparations on the boat. I was up at sunrise and wandered down to the marina armed with an industrial strength coffee to check it out. It became apparent almost immediately, this was the most unsuitable marina anywhere in The Canaries, to try to moor an ocean rowing boat. I walked around the quayside to the head office and met Bruno the boss. He was very helpful and spoke very good English. He explained that even though I had booked and paid for a berth months earlier, the marina was completely full, the only space available for my boat was up against a rough sheer concrete wall. I would need to buy some giant fenders and a rope ladder as soon as possible.

The boat was delivered later that morning, a day earlier than planned which caught me out. This meant I had no opportunity to find a more suitable marina further down the coast. By lunchtime that day she was launched and tied up against this rough concrete wall. The excitement was palpable, people appearing from every direction to come and have a look, many showing grave doubt that *Atlantic Rower* would last more than ten minutes, when out at sea. A Romanian family with a yacht moored nearby helped me tie up along the sea wall. They quickly fathomed that my ability to tie any kind of knot wasn't what they might have expected from someone about to take on the Atlantic.

The following morning, I discovered that the marina was very tidal. My boat had been badly scratched on her port side. Throughout the night she had been rubbed up and down the raw concrete. Signpost Express on the Isle of Wight had already done a really great job wrapping *Atlantic Rower* in vinyl. They would not have been happy to see this damage. You can't buy fenders in Puerto Rico marina, so I took a cab over to a nearby fishing village. I managed to buy two of the biggest fenders I had ever seen (they would have been perfect for the Titanic), plus a rope ladder, so I could actually get aboard and start the final preparations.

I then spent the afternoon lazing by the hotel swimming pool, getting a few rays in, while armed with a large G & T. Having a bit of a suntan before you row an ocean is a good idea. It avoids the need to carry extra after-sun lotion, adding more weight to the boat. In the final event my boat weighed in at about 1.2 tonnes fully laden. I received a phone call that day from one of the other solo rowers, whom I had first met in La Gomera just over a year earlier. This chap was one of the fittest rowers I ever met; he was from Scandinavia. He had helped me a year earlier by marking one side of my oars with yellow reflective tape, so I could see clearly at night if the oars were set properly in the gates. He had spotted my name on the pending YB tracker website. He was almost speechless when he discovered that I was having another go!

Later that day I discovered a great place for supper just over the road from the marina. It was called Restaurante Don Quijote, run by a lady called Elsa (nothing to do with the lioness, in *Born Free*). She ensured I could be fed anytime it suited me, despite normally being fully booked. This was without doubt one of the best and friendliest restaurants in Gran Canaria and with a great wine list.

I've never been very good at filling in forms (nor writing books for that matter!). I was about to embark on an Adventure rather than a sponsored Challenge. The difference between the two is enormous. I didn't need to fill in any forms or worry about red tape and endless disclaimers. Now in my late sixties, I was able to skip all of this time-consuming nonsense. I had visited my dentist before departure and been given the heads up. Just before Christmas, my doctor told me that I had a bone chip floating inside my right knee cap and this needed to be removed urgently. I ignored that advice as it would have meant delaying my departure for at least three months. I had recently survived a close encounter with prostate cancer and I now felt better than ever for a bit of rowing.

Still on the subject of paperwork: I had been told that I had to be armed with an exit visa stamped in my passport before I departed by sea from the EU. You might think this would be an easy thing to arrange. On Monday 9th January, I decided to pop up the road, find an immigration officer and get an exit visa. I wasn't actually planning to depart by boat for almost another week. Not knowing where to begin I visited my friend Bruno at the marina head office. He explained that there was nobody in the town who had the authority to furnish me with this passport exit stamp. Sometimes, maybe once a month, a Spanish official would call in and hand out these exit visas, but it was very doubtful this would happen again anytime soon. He suggested I should visit the main Police headquarters; they had an office in Maspalomas, about a 30-minute taxi ride. I arrived a little later that morning at the National Police HQ, feeling slightly anxious. Word had already been received: this Englishman was about to row alone across the ocean. Roman, the Chief of Police, was the most important Spanish gentleman I had ever met. He didn't ever want me to leave Maspalomas, let alone try to row the Atlantic Ocean… After much discussion he told me that the only man in Gran Canaria who could issue this exit visa, worked out of a tiny office around the back of the port of Las Palmas. He gave me directions and ordered a taxi to take me on another 40-minute drive to meet him.

On arrival in Las Palmas, it took another hour to locate his small office. Prior to leaving England I had been given an enormous list of paperwork. I had been told that without this, the local immigration authorities would not allow me to row out of Spain. I had spent days of my time assembling a massive *résumé* of rowing experience, a training log book, SSR and boat papers, insurance papers, VHF licences, sea survival & first aid certificates from two years earlier, plus a whole lot more. In the event none of this was required – the man in the office just wanted my passport. A few minutes later it had been stamped with his exit visa. I felt like I had just climbed Mt Everest, without a sherpa by my side. An hour later my taxi dropped me back at the Puerto Rico marina; I was exhausted but happy. The following day I carried on making final preparations and tried to write a list of where everything was located on the boat. I figured that in an emergency this would be a useful list to have, especially if there was a big drama during a storm at sea.

Fast forward to Wednesday 11th January. I had not had the opportunity to test my Schenker water maker since it had been serviced by the boatyard in Essex a year earlier. To test a water maker you need clear seawater, without any oil or grease floating on the surface. I checked with Jim in Weston-super-Mare. The water in the marina was clear, he felt it would be fine to run an early morning test. This would turn out to be the best decision I made during the final days of preparation. The moment I turned the machine on, water spurted out of a plastic nut between the main filter and the incoming water pipe. Had I allowed this to continue, the comms cabin would have been completely flooded in less than an hour. I concluded that when the water maker had been serviced and the filters changed, the plastic nut must have been accidentally over tightened. This had caused a hairline crack in the incoming sea water pipe. To make things worse still, the 'O' ring in the five micron secondary filter had been crushed. This caused water to leak profusely from the filter lid. Initially I was relieved that I had discovered this prior to departure. I hoped that I could find a plumbing shop somewhere in Gran Canaria, where they spoke some English and could supply me with the spare parts. This was wishful thinking, I visited at least 15 plumbing shops all over the island, without any success. After a whole day wasted and in the knowledge that this part was not metric, but of an imperial size, I had no chance ever of being able to fix it without outside help. I decided to call Jim again the following morning. The man was and is a complete legend, he knows more about making fresh water out of sea water than anyone else on the planet. When I called him on Thursday, he was in his car driving to Plymouth to visit a client. He pulled into a lay-by while I explained the problem. He immediately offered to return to his workshop, build me a completely new filtration unit that day, then offered to drive the parts himself to Gatwick Airport. This was after-sales service on a completely different scale… I thanked him, called EasyJet and managed to get the next flight to Gatwick, departing early that afternoon from Las Palmas.

I was slightly concerned about what might happen if there was an overly indulgent immigration officer on duty at passport control. If they had really checked my passport, they would have noticed that I had already departed Gran Canaria by boat! My stamped and dated exit visa out of the country, from just two days earlier, was there for everyone to see and I was really proud of it. Luckily the officer had a short attention span, he waved me through showing very little interest, alongside hundreds of other tanned tourists on afternoon flights. On arrival at Gatwick, Jim was just driving into the South terminal carpark with the main spare filter parts. He was also carrying several other spares which he felt I might require. To this day I have never experienced service quite like this. If you ever need a new water maker, advice or assistance, he is the only man to contact. I caught the next flight back out to Las Palmas and spent the day on Friday fitting the new filtration unit. A few hours later, I turned it on and *Hallelujah* it worked like a dream. I had learnt a cardinal lesson: learn how to service your water maker yourself, don't rely on anyone else unless it's Jim. Without a water maker, I would have been right up the creek without a paddle. I would most probably have been well out to sea before discovering the problem.

I was now almost ready to depart. I discovered from a great friend in Gurnard, that the annual ARC sailing race to the Caribbean was due to start this weekend from Las Palmas. She kindly offered to ensure that all of these yachties knew in advance, to be on the lookout for a solo rower somewhere near the island. I eventually decided that it would be better not to have 30 huge yachts up my transom, so soon after my departure. Instead, I would start my row on Monday 16th January 2023 in the early morning, irrespective of the prevailing weather. During that final weekend on terra firma, I had long telephone calls with all of my family. We had decided months earlier it was best that I was alone for the final preparations. Much more fun for any family members, to come over to the Caribbean for my arrival, rather than hang around for my departure. Technically, this could easily have been delayed and might have felt like a sad moment, waving goodbyes to each other.

Throughout all the final preparations to my *sequel*, we told very few people that I was planning to have another go. I didn't want that extra pressure on my family nor myself, with everyone trying to talk me out of the idea. For this reason, very early on my departure day, I only sent out a couple of emails to friends. The theme being, that by the time they read this email alert, I would already be at sea. They would have no opportunity to reply by email or phone, for possibly the next 90 days or more. They could, however, follow my voyage on a YB tracking device, which I had attached to my little boat. Meanwhile the support from my beautiful wife was unwavering, despite the heightened levels of stress my adventure must have caused her. Solid as a rock, she was to tell a wider group of friends and Red Squirrel supporters what I was up to. But only after I had rowed past the Cape Verde Islands, in a few weeks' time.

Late on Sunday afternoon my penultimate day on land, I remembered to visit the local Udaco supermarket to load up with fresh fruit and cheese. I knew that these would only last for maybe a week at sea. They would certainly be more exciting rations than dried food for every meal during my first few days on the Atlantic. I also remembered that a friend in Fishbourne had suggested I should take powdered milk, to add to hot drinks like coffee and tea. I added some Jacob's crackers to go with the cheese and paid the bill. I wandered back down to the boat and started to load these final provisions into the hatches on the rowing deck. I considered that under the water line they would remain much cooler than in the cabin.

Just as I was closing down for the evening, with the knowledge that I had done everything I could to be prepared, a very nice Bavarian lady from a nearby yacht came over. She spoke calmly at first with a slight German accent: 'Simon, you must not depart from here tomorrow.' Slightly dazed, I looked at her and asked why on earth not? Her voice became anxious and then she told me the reason. She and her husband had been mooring their yacht annually in Puerto Rico marina for the past 15 years. She knew everybody who was anybody here. They were friends with the local fishermen, marina workers and even the municipal street cleaners. She had been told that a Spanish bookmaker in the town, was making a price with good odds on my success or failure. The wager being offered revolved around the belief that I would be back in the marina, having given up, within less than ten days of my departure. You could gamble on the number of days I might survive in the ocean! I suggested to her that she should immediately place a bet on me never coming back, at least not this year.

I asked why these locals were all so confident that I would give up, after such a short time at sea. Her explanation stunned me. The fishermen knew the weather forecast was so dire for the next week that they themselves had decided to stay put in the marina. I was only to discover later, that these guys did understand the local weather and I probably should have heeded their advice... But I had already made my decision, I was rowing out at 08.00 hrs, tomorrow morning, and I expected them all to lose their money.

SIX

The Departure

M onday 16th January, I awoke around 05.00 hrs. Dived into the shower, for what would be my final visit to a bathroom for several months, then checked out of the hotel. The staff had all been very efficient and it had been the ideal place to stay. A few cockerels were letting rip as the sun rose early in the eastern sky. As I walked out past the swimming pool, a couple of guests were sipping coffee and having breakfast. I had never met them before but one of them turned to me and asked the innocent question, 'Are you going down to the beach?' I replied, 'No… I'm just going off to row the Atlantic.' They gave me the strangest look; it was really quite funny and made me smile…

It was quiet and calm in the marina. I was very excited, the big day had arrived and clearly the fishermen in the marina knew nothing about nothing. There wasn't even a light breeze. The nice Bavarian lady who had warned me the day before not to go out, was on hand, and she had arranged for a couple of locals to guide me out of the marina, following their small rubber inflatable boat. This was good practice, just to ensure that I wouldn't smash into other moored yachts with my extended oars. At exactly 07.59 hrs, I shouted to a bystander, 'Ropes away', he did the necessary and got to keep my old rope ladder in recompense.

Soon after 08.10 hrs, I was rowing out of the marina and into the Atlantic Ocean, feeling very happy that my adventure had begun. I knew I needed to get as far away from the land as quickly as possible, to ensure I wouldn't be blown back onto the rocks if the wind decided to get up.

Before my departure I had hired the services of a senior meteorologist, whose name was also Simon, and he was to text me daily weather updates. Many of his text messages would feature in my ship's log. We never had a good reason to speak on my satellite phone or by telephone for that matter. Except for once, months earlier, when I had called him to ask if he would take on this task. Suffice to say he was completely brilliant at his job. So good in fact, that I had been told that a certain rugby team always hired his services, before they played at Twickenham. They needed to be sure, in the event they won the toss, that they always picked the best end of the pitch for the kick off. This might not be true, but it's a good story anyway!

With enormous difficulty, I had managed to pair my Apple iPhone to my Garmin GPS. The keyboard on the Apple device is significantly easier to use than that on the Garmin. In high seas and on a rocking boat, I was able to type faster and more accurately on the iPhone. Messages were then sent via the Garmin on the Global Iridium satellite network. Those I contacted could reply to my texts at no cost to themselves.

As well as immediate family, Simon my meteorologist and the US Coastguard, I added the contact details of a small group of friends, whom I could contact for technical advice. Some of these experts are referred to throughout the voyage as 'the Commodore', 'the Captain', 'the Lieutenant' and 'the Midshipman'; I was 'the Rower'. I should mention here, the naval ranks mentioned throughout later chapters are entirely fictious: nicknames, and not to be confused with the real thing. It is highly unlikely that these friends would have ever passed into Britannia Royal Naval College!

Trying to physically write a log on *Atlantic Rower* would have been almost impossible. With the constant movement of the boat, it often felt like I was inside a tumble dryer. The voice memo App on my iPhone provided the solution. I made daily recordings of my adventure. On my return I would transcribe hours of dictation, and use this as a very accurate account of my voyage, from which to write this book. For this reason, parts of my log are deliberately written in the *present* tense.

By 09.30 hrs, I had rowed out to sea sufficiently far from land to stop and have a cup of coffee, using my gas Jet boil. This cooker was very small, it used an Isobutane/Propane fuel mix and was able to boil water for a cup of tea in under 60 seconds. Manufactured strictly for outdoor use, it became a lethal weapon if not treated with extreme care in high seas! Naked flames on boats can be very dangerous. I had made a special holder for the small gas canister on the deck and rarely turned it on inside the cabin. Written in large writing on the gas cannister were the words 'Fuel Bigger Adventures'. This seemed very appropriate for what I was trying to do.

I enjoyed a light breeze as I departed and still couldn't understand why the local fishermen were behaving like wimps, staying safe in the marina. By the time I stopped rowing for elevenses, the wind was blowing at 15–20 knots from the east and the swell had increased to about 3m. I carried on rowing throughout the rest of the day, only stopping briefly for water or a snack. Sometime during that first afternoon I tried calling up a passing boat called 'Yasser *something*'. I had picked her up on my AIS system, but the skipper didn't answer his radio and fortunately they eventually passed about 200m behind me without incident.

By early evening on that first day, I needed a proper rest. The wind was still being influenced by the Island's topography or to give it the correct technical name, the 'Island's shadow'. It had swung around, so that it was now blowing from the SE at 10 knots. I was somewhere between the islands of Gran Canaria and Tenerife, and at 23.00 hrs my exact position was 27° 39' N, 15° 58' W.

I was now drifting with my hand steering ropes cleated off at midships. I decided to try to have a snooze and thought to myself: 'It's Goodnight from him and it's Goodnight from her'.

During that first night at sea, I didn't dare attempt to lie down in the sleeping cabin. I spent most of the early hours watching out for land as I was still being pushed gradually north by the stiff breeze. I knew at first light the forecast was for the wind to change direction, to blow from the ENE at around 15 knots. My first 24 hours at sea had been successful, I had rowed about 40nm. For my own sanity, days at sea would always start at 08.00 hrs UTC. They would end at 07.59.59 hrs UTC the following morning. This was because I had commenced my row at 08.00 hrs UTC on Monday morning. Throughout the next 70-plus days, all times referred to are denominated in UTC. I only switched time zones to UTC minus 4 very near the completion of my voyage, when I refer to 'local time' in the Caribbean. While I didn't know it then, UTC means Universal Time Coordinated. Prior to 1972, this time was known as Greenwich Mean Time (GMT) and some people now prefer to call it Zulu time.

Day two, Simon had texted me soon after sunrise. He advised that there was a low-pressure system coming my way early next week. I would be well advised to stay east, rowing relatively near the coast of West Africa. Anything to avoid getting caught up in that cyclone. The Cape Verde Islands were still 900 miles south of my current position. Everything was going well on the boat and nothing had broken yet. I was feeling quite pleased with myself and sent text messages to Sara and each of our children. I assured them that I was safe and well, they had absolutely nothing to worry about. Since departing on the row, I had seen no wildlife with the exception of a couple of errant seagulls. No fish, and unlike my aborted start of a year earlier, no killer whales – or orcas as they are more commonly known. This was a huge relief, but I still hoped to catch a glimpse of normal whales someday, somewhere in the Atlantic, sometime soon.

When I did stop rowing at around 14.00 hrs, I set up lunch in my comms cabin. I couldn't help thinking to myself, everything out here is so completely different, why on earth am I doing this? I must be completely nuts. Hopefully I won't feel like this by the time I arrive on the other side. For now, it was a great way to get fit. The true benefits of not having to take or make phone calls all day long, read text messages, reply to WhatsApps and email, without access to Wi-Fi and the internet, had not yet sunk in. The reality of life out in the big wide world is frequently really grim. I wasn't missing having to watch the carnage the Russians were imposing on Ukraine. I wasn't missing the waffle from British politicians about Covid or campervans, before some of them got caught out with their pants down. I knew that I would be hearing no news at all until I arrived on the other side and this was a great feeling. I decided very early on, that if I was ever very wealthy, I would start a 'Good News Channel'. To be aired at the same time as existing nightly news broadcasts, just to ensure that the great British public had something to smile about every day. One of the highlights after a long day on the oars was being able to eat delicious cheese on a Jacob's cracker, followed by a fresh banana.

Day three, I had rowed 91nm in the first 48 hours, which I felt was not too bad for a beginner and a grandpa. My weather forecaster texted me before breakfast, now showing greater anxiety regarding the rapidly developing low-pressure system. Suggesting I should now row as they do in the Oxford -v- Cambridge boat race. The only similarity between *Atlantic Rower* and these university rowing boats was that they both shared exactly the same type of rollocks. I needed to row my bum off, day and night, to try to get further south to avoid the need to deploy my para-anchor. A sea anchor, or para-anchor, is similar to a large parachute on a 70m rope. You only use it when you are being blown backwards by the wind or being pushed backwards by a strong adverse current. They are a real pain in the backside to rein in onboard a rowing boat once they are no longer required. They become saturated and you really need the whole thing to dry properly on the rowing deck, before it can be properly stored in the aft cabin. I had already decided that I would do everything in my power, to avoid ever having to use this piece of kit.

After a delicious lunch, I decided the moment had come to run my water maker. The sun was still high in the sky, meaning that power loss from using the water maker would soon be replenished via the solar panels. To my amazement it worked absolutely perfectly. In less than 45 minutes I had filled both of my ten litre plastic jerry cans. I felt this was a good decision given the dodgy weather forecast for later that week. Running a water maker uses more power from the lithium batteries on a rowing boat than everything else put together. The old saying, 'Make hay while the sun shines', was very appropriate.

On my third night at sea, I didn't get a lot of sleep as I must have rowed or drifted into a major shipping lane. My AIS alarm went off twice during the night and the sea state was growing bigger by the minute. The first close encounter caused me to call a passing ship on my portable radio, asking the skipper to politely buzz off. The second dodged bullet happened a few hours later in complete darkness, a cargo freighter called Cap San Raphael. The skipper of this boat was very friendly and while he told me that I was not appearing on his AIS system, he eventually passed well in front of my bow doing about 20 knots. This made me feel rather jealous, given my maximum speed to date had only been around 2.5 knots.

Day four, breakfast was delicious, it's getting too rough out here to use the Jet boil. I don't want to spill it all over myself ending up with third degree burns. Instead, I started off with a can of Jimmy's iced coffee, just to ensure that sleep deprivation wasn't going to spoil my day. I then polished off a mixed berry meal using cold water. I felt as if I had just consumed two very rare Big Macs, I was completely re-energised for the day ahead. As I finished breakfast, I heard the ping of an incoming text. My meteorologist was pleased with my speed and course. The wind speed and direction over the next few days would be predominantly from the NNE at 20 knots. To avoid the worst of the impending cyclone, I should keep aiming south towards the Cape Verde Islands and don't hang around. He asked if the Big Green Monster had left the boat. I had no idea what he was talking about. I replied that we both shared a great Christian name, but had I missed something with the BGM? He immediately replied, 'Seasickness.' It was only then that I realised this had not been a problem at all. I was religiously taking one 15mg Stugeron tablet with a multivitamin pill daily; clearly this was working a treat. The only time I ever felt seasick on *Atlantic Rower* was during that training episode, when I was caught out with my pants down (so to speak), off the St Catherine's Lighthouse near Ventnor. The only other supplements which I took along with me were Vitamin B12 tablets. These are meant to help you stop getting cramps; well, I haven't had any cramps so those seem to have worked fine too.

Before I departed, Sara had given me something similar to a Villeroy & Boch loo. Slightly more comfortable than a bucket, but with a similar flush mechanism. *Bucket and chuck it, and check the wind direction first.* On calm days at sea this worked a treat, but when the waves became enormous, not so easy. Trying to do what I was trying to do was akin to landing a wildcat helicopter, onto the aft deck of a destroyer in a storm.

In between rowing for my life, I received several text messages from home. Winter was in full swing, frost on the ground and it was freezing. Everything in our garden was white. I replied that I hoped everything was okay and that my row should be over soon, just another 60, 70 or maybe 100 days. I didn't know for sure but I'm going to carry on, carrying on. Support from home came in different guises. Not only by satellite text, but to my surprise, I discovered a secret stash of handwritten and typed notes from a wider group of very good friends. What I hadn't taken in, was that Sara had packed these notes into each one of my 85 daily ration bags. This had been done without my knowledge, just prior to my departure over a year earlier from La Gomera. I was using the same ration bags now as from my previous attempt. I was soon to discover that these extraordinary messages of support and encouragement, would have a very positive effect on my mental state throughout the crossing.

Today I saw three different birds of two different gull species, a bit like swallows but slightly bigger. I am now over 200 miles from the coast of Africa, it's quite exciting to see these birds flying around and coming to check out my rowing boat. I still haven't seen a single fish. As the sea state grew ever larger, I adjusted the height of my oars in the rollocks (row gates) to compensate for this. I could now power on, full speed ahead with greater ease.

I had no set daily rowing routine, for the reason I thought that this could become very boring, very quickly. I had spoken with and read stories of previous solo ocean rowers who felt a routine was an essential for survival out here. But like with so many other things, I simply didn't get this. I decided before I set off that I would row and rest exactly when I wanted to. Some days I would row for two hours and then rest for 30 minutes. Other days I would row for three hours and then rest for an hour. If I was really knackered, then maybe I would spoil myself and snooze for two or three hours. In summary, I had decided that I would just go with the flow, and stop or start whenever it suited me. I wasn't out here trying to prove anything to anyone else, I just wanted to row an ocean. Today would be a long one, I was on the oars for almost 18 hours. With short rests every three hours, I stuck to this until sunrise on day five of my mission.

The incoming text at 08.00 hrs, told me that I had covered 63nm which made the extra effort overnight feel all worthwhile. I was flying. Simon even suggested to me that I should stand by to stand by, as I think he was equally surprised. Our son made contact: Glad to hear that all is well and glad to hear that you're using **that** toothbrush. Many years earlier Doug1(correct spelling!), had attended our son's 21st birthday party in France. He had given all of us very smart new and engraved toothbrushes. These had been manufactured by his parents' family business. Here I was, using this same toothbrush, still as good as new almost ten years later! I thought to myself, this could be one of the greatest product endorsements in history. Now the toothbrush would be tested to its limit in these harsh Atlantic conditions!

'The Lieutenant' texted to let me know that over the past five days, I had rowed the equivalent of ten marathons. I replied that he was probably the only person I knew who would understand what it feels like surfing a one-tonne rowing boat in a 12m swell. I also confirmed to him that I had not gone completely bananas yet. I asked him to relay a message to Bothways & Talkie that I was enjoying Campari and Sodas for sundowners most evenings and that all was well. This was clearly nonsense. Soon after this exchange I recorded on my voice memo, 'It's pretty wild out here today, not that windy but the waves seem to be significantly bigger than anything I've experienced so far. In fact, it's a bit like going through blocks of huge skyscrapers, it's exciting because they overtake the boat.'

It was just starting to drizzle for the first time since I had set off. Simon told me that he was now copying Sara into the daily weather forecasts. I thought this was a great idea, so long as he wasn't forecasting a hurricane or anything similar! I had agreed with Sara before my departure that I wouldn't be sending her any bad news by text. For the reason neither she nor anyone else would be able to help if I got into real difficulty. I certainly didn't wish for her to worry any more than she might have been already. As the day progressed, I speculated as to why older ships like HMS Victory had a poop deck. While this name had originated from the French word for a stern, *la poupe*, it could easily have described something completely different. Trying to do one of these in enormous seas, hanging onto the grab rails for dear life and trying to keep the loo paper dry, was one hell of an achievement. I decided that if the waves continued the way they were at the moment, then I might have to 'hold on' and cut these down to once every three days. This would have been very uncomfortable!

Given the wild conditions I decided to row several long shifts throughout the night. When I did lie down for a 30-minute snooze, I concluded that it was actually quite cold. I pulled myself into the mummy-shaped sleeping bag. This was a bad idea; I had been advised the previous year that the Americans manufactured some sort of sleeping cover, which you just threw over your body. Every time my AIS alarm sounded warning of an imminent collision, it just became a big hassle to get out of the sleeping bag.

I should mention here that as a solo rower, when you need to eat or sleep, you simply lock off the rudder with ropes at midships and hope it drifts in the right direction – 50% of the time this seemed to work, the rest of the time the boat would drift sideways or backwards, meaning lost mileage.

Day six and the weekend at last. I had already received my daily weather text. I was the fastest row boat in the East Atlantic right now; this made me laugh. My hopes were raised by Simon's suggestion that there was at last a real chance of missing that weather front. It was still coming my way but he would let me know how that developed over the weekend. I replied to him 'Brilliant news, congratulations on being the best meteorologist on the planet', and he immediately responded, 'See if you say that in a month'!

I decided that the only reason I still hadn't seen any whales, sharks, or any other fish for that matter, was entirely due to the size of the swell and the waves. They were almost certainly right underneath my little boat and circling me.

Trying to give an accurate assessment of wave size is extremely difficult with the naked eye. I knew my boat was 25-foot long and when I went up the front of these waves the distance was at least double the length of the boat. Thus, 50-foot waves seemed to be quite normal out here today. However, the best way I can describe wave height with any semblance of accuracy, is to explain what happened to my plastic mineral water bottle. Most people reading this will have been up in an aeroplane at some time in their lives. You will all know what happens to a plastic water bottle which is only half full of water, as you climb or descend in the plane. To get wave height into perspective, this was now happening to my plastic water bottle on the rowing deck... The change in atmospheric pressure between the top and bottom of these waves was so great, that it caused my plastic bottle to expand and decompress on each movement. This doesn't happen in calm seas, so I can state without a shadow of doubt, these waves were absolutely huge.

For the rest of the day there was some rain and several wild waves. One of these slammed into the side of the boat so hard, that my hydraulic autohelm was knocked out of the socket in the aft cabin. An alarm sounded and a message in the comms cabin told me that the autohelm had been disconnected. I felt this was very impressive as the alarm hadn't ever sounded before. I was slightly nervous; I knew I needed to open the aft cabin hatch in these big seas to check if there was a real problem. To enter the aft cabin, I needed to be almost horizontal and crawl in to have a look. I knew that if a wave landed on the rowing deck during the process, then this would be chips. The only lesson I had learnt from all my training in the North Sea and around the Isle of Wight, was that both these hatches must be kept firmly closed at all times. If water entered either cabin, then there was a real chance that the boat would not self-right. If a rogue wave caused *Atlantic Rower* to capsize, I would be finished. I soon discovered that my brand new autohelm had a steel pin holding it securely to the aft cabin shelf. Somehow this had come loose. It took me some time as waves crashed over the boat to find this small pin. Eventually I managed to get back to the comms cabin to try to mend it. I could now turn the alarm off, which by now was driving me up the wall. I tried pushing the pin back into position, but worked out that this problem would almost certainly reoccur, unless it could be permanently fixed.

I made a call on my satellite phone to a marine electrician. A couple of years earlier, I had done an expensive electrical course with him ahead of the Challenge. In one hour, he had taught me more about electrics than I had learnt in my entire life! He worked at the boatyard and was still at work when I called. He was really helpful, pointing out that this same problem had happened in the past. I do remember thinking to myself, if the same problem had happened in the past, why hadn't I been told this earlier? The best solution was to use a thin strip of Gorilla tape and wrap it around the unit after I had re-inserted the steel pin. Ten minutes later job done, I decided to use the other brand new hydraulic arm, with tape attached. It worked and despite the sea state, only a small amount of water had entered the aft cabin while I was in there, trying to find my reading glasses!

As darkness enveloped the boat, the stars came out for what was to be one of those fantastic shooting star spectacles. Well away from land in the Atlantic Ocean, I had already discovered that there was no light pollution. The stars looked completely stunning every night, except when the sky was obscured by fog or cloud. I simply can't explain just how really beautiful it is. Bored with night time rowing sometimes, I would simply lean back on my rowing seat and watch the fireworks above me... This in conjunction with occasional bioluminescent plankton in the water, as I pulled on the oars, made my adventure even more exhilarating.

Day seven, Sunday morning at sea and all's well. My early morning weather text pinged; it emboldened me with the news that I was still the fastest row boat in the East Atlantic. I should expect more Cumulus cloud throughout the day and NE winds at 10-15 knots. With a bit of luck, I should miss the worst of the weather front. I'm still hoping I won't need to deploy my para-anchor. At this time of the morning the sea state looks similar to scrambled eggs. There is no clear wave direction and the boat is being thrown from left to right as a light shower of rain lands on my head. Still no fish, but I know that they must be out here somewhere. I'm expecting one morning soon, I will open my eyes and find the boat is surrounded by a Noah's Ark of sea creatures. Whales, dolphins, blue marlin and maybe a few sharks thrown in for good measure.

I'm still a good six to seven days north of the Cape Verde Islands. There is an old nautical saying, 'Head south until the butter melts and then turn west'. Well, my butter hasn't shown any inclination to melt just yet, this despite the increased daily temperature as I head further south into the Tropics. If everything goes to plan the Trade winds should cut in when the butter has melted. At that point I need to turn hard to starboard and start rowing across the main body of the Atlantic Ocean. I'm so excited by this thought that I have placed a small paddy of butter on the rowing deck. I now spend much of my time on the oars just watching it.

As I rowed on south, I reflected on the fact I should have nicked (borrowed) a couple more beach towels from the hotel in Gran Canaria. It was now raining quite hard and everything was getting well and truly soaked. Attempting to dry anything in these conditions was completely impossible. By tea time I had rowed about 19nm since breakfast. This included getting some help from the swell and using the boat as a surf board. The waves around the boat are now enormous, in my opinion even bigger than large skyscrapers. On many occasions my little boat was being carried forward by over 60m on these huge rolling waves. I was laughing to myself, whilst this was very exhilarating, I was also completely out of control during the ride. I called home yesterday and spoke to Sara along with both my daughters. I'll call my son this evening and give him a complete update.

SEVEN

Storms

Day eight, Monday morning loomed and long before breakfast, I was awoken in the sleeping cabin at 05.27 hrs. The boat was hit by the biggest rogue wave you could ever possibly imagine. The enormous crash on the roof of the boat scared the hell out of me, I felt as though it had been hit by a train. The boat went over by almost 180°, I was completely upside down. The entire contents of the sleeping cabin landed on top of me. Some of the electronics had gone down and my ears rang to the tune of alarms. I yanked myself out of my sleeping bag as the boat slowly righted herself. It was pitch-black outside on the rowing deck. The first thought that came to my mind was thank heavens I hadn't actually seen this coming in slow motion. I had no idea what damage may have been caused to the boat and opted to stay inside the cabin until the sun came up. I managed to restore the power to my autohelm and turn off the alarms. I made myself a cup of coffee, carefully, so as not to spill boiling water all over myself. I remember thinking and just hoping there was no material damage to either the structure of the boat nor the solar panels on both roofs. These were essential to my life out here in the middle of nowhere.

I knew it would be at least another hour or so before I could do a proper inspection at first light. I consoled myself with the ridiculous idea that whatever was broken I should be able to fix it myself. I shone my Toro flashlight through the cabin hatch window and saw that everything on the row deck had been completely re-arranged. I wasn't prepared to investigate in the darkness, in case the boat should be clobbered again by another rogue wave. As the new day dawned, I was astonished to discover that my little boat appeared to have survived this massive onslaught. It was several more days before I worked out that my brand-new anemometer, which sits on top of the aft mast, had been completely saturated underwater when the boat had gone over. On completing a thorough inspection of the boat, I discovered that the wave had hit the deck so hard, it had cracked all of the plastic rims on my four circular deck hatches. These contained my rations and were now leaking. This despite being screwed into and glued onto the actual deck, they had all been broken by the force of the water.

The daily text update from Simon started, 'Definitely the fastest rowboat in the East Atlantic today!' At the end of his message, 'Hopefully you'll be able to stay off para-anchor now and hope all's well'. I replied to him explaining that the boat had never been on para-anchor but had been seriously clobbered. 'There don't appear to be any leeks in the boat.' He replied: 'Stray Welsh veggies have no place on board.' I blamed my Apple for that typo.

After devouring a hot breakfast, I did the calculation. Seventy nautical miles rowed in the previous 24 hours, albeit with a bit of help from some surfing, meant an average speed of almost three knots. Even the fittest four-man rowing teams in the annual Challenge rarely achieved this performance. I was really pleased with myself, though I was never to achieve that many nautical miles again, in any 24-hour period during my crossing. I have rowed exactly 413nm in my first week at sea and had been scared silly on more than one occasion by the sheer size of the waves!

After a mid-morning rain storm, the sun broke through and it wasn't long before I had almost completely forgotten about the early morning dramas. I decided to treat myself and have a hot lunch, washed down with a very large gin and tonic, to celebrate surviving my first **critical incident**. After lunch, I noted that my hands, now covered in blisters, were becoming quite ugly. I strapped them up with rowing tape, in the hope it might make rowing slightly less painful. By the following day I removed the tape and decided to wear row gloves. Thin chamois leather with the fingers cut out, this seemed like a huge improvement as I knew that I still had a very long way to go. By early evening I was exhausted; I dozed off for a few hours; tomorrow would be another day and I was still alive.

Day nine and one week and a day since I set to sea, leaving the comforts of the marina in Gran Canaria behind me. It had been another wild night with waves crashing over the top of the boat on multiple occasions. My autohelm had become disconnected twice in the darkness. It's a bit scary when this happens as I have no control over the direction of the boat in the water. As the big waves come powering in, the boat then gets broadsided and risks being knocked down again or capsized. My forecast was for a cloudy day with little sunshine. Winds from the ENE at 10-15 knots would drop off to below eight knots over the coming few days. I felt that the huge seas I had just been through would also calm down a bit. This turned out to be wishful thinking on my part.

I was hoping to get much closer this week to the Cape Verde Islands and was dreaming of watching that butter melt. As I rowed on throughout the day, I spotted the first of what I initially thought might be a flying fish. In fact, on closer inspection, it appeared to have a kind of sail in the form of a balloon. It looked very enticing, coloured in beautiful shades of violet and blue. The top of the balloon feature was floating 4-5 inches above the sea. I had read that these jellyfish named Portuguese men of war can kill humans, so opted not to go swimming.

Later that afternoon I decided to get some food out of the forward deck hatch. From the outside it appeared to have cracked more than the others during the recent storm. As I unscrewed the lid, I immediately realised that the entire food locker was more than 75% flooded with sea water. For so much water to have entered this compartment, it could only have happened yesterday, during the time the boat had been completely inverted. This was another **critical incident**. Given it was too late in the day to do anything about it, I decided another triple G & T was the only solution for now. I would tackle the problem at first light tomorrow.

My fresh food supplies from the supermarket in Gran Canaria were now running low, the remaining bananas starting to go brown, the apples getting softer and the cheese starting to smell awful. This evening would be the last day eating fruit and cheese, although I still had some Jacob's crackers for emergencies… I was completely exhausted after days of huge seas and felt that by the end of today, I should spoil myself and try to get a proper night's sleep. I had two small alarm clocks in the sleeping cabin, one of which I normally set to wake me every 20 minutes. While snoozing, I needed to check my chart plotter regularly for other ships in the area, just to ensure I wasn't about to collide with them. I turned this alarm off and I slept for the best part of five hours and awoke feeling like a new man. Nothing had disturbed me except the sound of waves broadsiding me and crashing onto the row deck.

Day ten, the early morning ping from an incoming text awoke me. My meteorologist explained that while the weather front to my west was sucking in air, the wind was now dying. He expected it to be a cloudy day and as usual this proved to be correct. He suggested that I would be dragged in a westerly direction as the full effect of this weather front took hold. I should do my best to keep rowing south as far as possible. I had omitted to tell him or Sara that *Atlantic Rower* was now listing heavily on her port side. Rowing was becoming difficult due to the fact the boat was heavily laden with sea water, in both of the port food lockers. While trying to row, my starboard oar regularly completely missed the water and my port oar was considerably lower in the water than it should have been. Rowing boats need to be weighted and balanced in perfect equilibrium. I was not quite rowing in a clockwise circle, but had to compensate the whole time just to keep her on a straight course. As the sun rose in the east, I knew the moment had come to sort out this problem.

The first thing I needed to do, was remove the life raft from the centre of the boat. Inside that compartment were bungs and I figured that if I could remove these, then the water should flow out towards the electric bilge pump in the centre of the boat. The sea was still quite choppy and as I removed the life raft using the two detachable slings, I realised just how heavy it was. Weighing about 35kg normally, it now felt more like 50kg due to the fact it had become partially saturated. Having removed it, I then managed to get at the bungs to ensure the water flowed into this chamber, before flowing on towards the bilge pump. Success! I switched on the electric bilge pump and it worked a treat, sea water was pouring out over the side of the boat.

The next job was to get almost 37% of my water-logged rations out of the small hatch and onto the deck, so they might start to dry out. There isn't exactly a lot of space on a solo rowboat. The rowing deck is just over two metres in length and possibly only one metre wide to allow the gunwales to function effectively. While the sea state grew in intensity, I loaded more and more food bags into a huge pile on the deck. I felt I should also check the smaller food compartment, located at the aft on the port side. This too had been half flooded. It meant more food removal so that I could access another bung to drain out that sea water. This may sound simple but it wasn't. The boat started lurching to the starboard side due to the weight of all the food bags, many of which were now contaminated with sea water. By midday I had completely drained both hatches, I had dried as much of the food that could be saved. I then spent some time on my head trying to ensure the food compartments were dry, using one of those towels which I had borrowed from the hotel.

I had one final visual check just to ensure that my hull had not been pierced by a marlin or damaged in any other way. I could hardly believe just how much water had entered both hatches. Marlin strikes on ocean rowing boats were becoming quite commonplace by the end of 2022. Being speared by the sword of a blue marlin travelling at 40mph plus, was not something to take lightly. I had heard and seen photographs of a chap in a four-man boat. He had been in the sleeping cabin, horizontal with his legs slightly apart. A blue marlin sword pierced the hull underneath him and had come to rest about six inches inside the cabin floor, in between his legs. His escape from sure death had been quite extraordinary. I had learnt that during the years prior to the pandemic, large cruise ships regularly threw excess food and rotting waste overboard. For the marlin this was a dream; they frequently followed these large ocean liners waiting for an easy meal. Soon after the arrival of Covid, with the risk of infectious contagion on board, most of these ships were laid up in ports for a couple of years. The biggest losers were the blue marlin – they had to look elsewhere at meal times. So it was, that over the next couple of years, more and more small boats were speared by marlin. The blue marlin mistook the white hulls of several ocean row boats for large tuna with serious consequences. I had been advised to consider laying Kevlar on the floor of my sleeping cabin. It is held to be about seven times stronger than steel. But for the reason it was heavy and would be difficult to attach, I opted to pass on this idea.

The sealed compartments were now bone dry. I replaced all the food bags which hadn't been contaminated with salt water, into the aft hatch, everything else into the forward hatch. I also decided that this forward hatch should now become my onboard dustbin for the rest of the trip. Whilst the bulk of my sealed wet and dry food bags had survived, almost 50% of my snack packs had to be chucked into the new onboard dustbin, completely waterlogged. I recognised that I might need to ration my daily intake of calories at some point down the track. It was too wet on the deck now to ensure all the hatches were properly sealed. I would use my whole supply of black Gorilla tape in the coming days, to create new seals around the cracked black plastic rims. For now, I used a special hatch spanner to completely tighten them all, this I figured would keep the water at bay until I could tape them up properly.

The final act before lunch that day seemed simple enough. All I had to do was ensure the slings were secure under the Seago 4-man life raft, then lift and lower it back into the centre compartment. Just at the critical moment as I lifted it, sod's law prevailed and I was broadsided by a large wave. One of the slings slipped out from under the 35kg container and the whole thing landed on my left foot. You know the feeling when you drop something heavy on your toes? Well this was considerably worse – had I broken a bone in my foot or not? Hobbling around, a few minutes later I managed to insert the life raft and closed the hatch. As I treated myself to another lamb with mint and rosemary lunch, I could visibly see my foot swelling. Pudding consisted of several Ibuprofen 400mg tablets and while the pain started to subside, my foot did not… It was time for another gin and tonic, another **critical incident** had been declared!

The boat was now completely surrounded by lethal Portuguese men of war jellyfish. I had been really efficient before departure and had packed a bottle of white vinegar just for this reason. I figured that it was quite within the realms of probability, that one of these creatures could be washed onto the deck at any time. I might even hook one with an oar during night time rowing and somehow get stung. In the event this never happened but it was good to be prepared. I had been waiting for a suitable day to jump in and scrub the barnacles off the hull. Many of these crustaceans had become attached in warm water during the fortnight *Atlantic Rower* had been moored up in Puerto Rico marina. I decided that there was no way I would be attempting this exercise anytime soon with all these lethal jellies around the boat.

I decided to stop feeling sorry for myself and get back into it, row, row, row the boat. Now that she lay in perfect equilibrium on the water, this proved a lot easier. I settled in on the oars with extreme pain in my left foot, still not knowing if it was broken or just badly bruised. The easterly wind continued to blow me further off course. I tried as hard as I could to row in a southerly direction. This was to be the only time when I seriously contemplated getting out my drogues. Drogues are a lot smaller than a para-anchor. You attach and trail them behind the transom, they look a bit like mini orange parachutes. The idea is that they slow you down as they fill up with water. They help give you a bit more stability when racing down waves. It was still completely wild out here but for the life of me, I couldn't remember exactly where I had stored them. I knew they were somewhere in the aft cabin but wasn't planning to risk a flood in there. I was never able to find them during my entire voyage, so I never got to use them.

I had fitted the boat with a Fusion waterproof speaker, easily removable from a puck on the outside bulkhead or when attached to another puck in the comms cabin. The speaker was paired to my iPhone. I had downloaded lots of great music from iTunes. These songs, coupled with several hundred Shazam tracks and very high volume, ensured I never got bored while rowing.

The music was just awesome. I stopped briefly for supper and continued to row on into the night, resting for a couple of hours whenever I felt completely stuffed.

Day 11, I was greeted by great news from Sara. She had calculated that I had just completed 568 nautical miles in ten days; the whole family was very excited. I felt as though I had survived a baptism of fire throughout these early days at sea, but nobody else knew of the real dramas. My left foot was now more swollen than ever, I carried on munching through lots of Ibuprofen. 'The Lieutenant' texted to say that I was now on the 22nd parallel North and approaching the Cape Verde area. He also wanted to remind me to watch out for an asteroid which was passing 2,100 miles away from our planet later today. It was the size of an elephant. In these conditions out here right now, this was the least of my worries!

Australia Day dawned; it was Thursday 26th January. Simon texted to tell me that I was the only boat now in the East Atlantic not to be on para-anchor. 'Well done,' he said; this made me laugh. I knew that most rowing boats on the Atlantic right now had departed 35 days before me in the 2022 Challenge. They would have been much further across the ocean than my tiny little boat. I had only rowed 48nm over the past 24 hours and was still being blown by the easterlies in the direction of the cyclone. I replied to Simon, 'Thank you but I'm about to be overtaken by a large cargo ship which is almost alongside, so better get on with it.'

Later that morning I used my Sat phone to call Geoff in Cowes. He is the best marine electrician on the Isle of Wight. For the past ten nights I had been blinded by the backlights on the deck repeaters. I'm sure this caused my eyeballs to revolve from time to time; they definitely needed to be dimmed. Geoff was stunned to hear from me. Clearly, he had either forgotten or didn't believe I could be so stupid as to attempt this row. This was despite the fact I had warned him recently, I was going to do it. As usual he was completely brilliant this small problem he solved in a matter of seconds, and it was to make my life a lot less stressful, especially during the hours of darkness.

It turned out to be the calmest day since I had set off. Perfect for applying the Gorilla tape to the broken black plastic rims under the deck hatches. I decided to play it safe and did a perfect job on all four, just in case the other two started to let seawater into the starboard food lockers. While I wouldn't recommend this ocean rowing for your next family holiday, I would suggest you should never leave home without Gorilla tape. It is quite likely that my little boat would have sunk without it.

By late that afternoon a lot more Portuguese men of war jellies had come by to greet me. Two or three birds which I hadn't seen before showed up and circled the boat. I tried to imagine if they might have just flown over 250 nautical miles from Mauritania to my east, or had they come up from the Cape Verde Islands to my south. Still no whales or sharks but from time to time a piece of plastic goes floating past the boat, dropped by somebody irresponsibly into the sea. I was absolutely appalled to see this, especially in such a beautiful place on our planet.

As I rowed on, I was already dreaming of my planned pit stop for supper. Having only yesterday reorganised most of my rations, I had come across a packet of wet food containing meatballs and pasta. I feared these could be really nasty having never tried them before. I dreamt of polishing off this meal with a bottle of Le Dome 2015, from Jonathan's Chateau in Bordeaux. I didn't carry a dinner gong on the boat, but the moment had arrived. I boiled up some water on my Jet boil and poured it into a small Pyrex glass dish on the rowing deck. I then slipped in the sealed packet of wet food and finally put on the plastic lid. This would warm up the food and gave me ample time to find a cork screw and ensure the wine wasn't corked. Somebody very wise (it could have been Uncle Andrew) once said that you should always travel with two corkscrews. When asked why, the reason given was: just in case you lost one of them. Armed with this knowledge I always carried three of them on the rowing boat.

I don't wish to get too carried away about the dinner, but it was simply delicious. Congratulations to Wayfayrer for a great meal and thank you, Jonathan, for the excellent wine. Le Dome 2010 had been given 100 points by Robert Parker; at the time this was the pinnacle of their endeavours at Chateau Teyssier. They were suddenly up there as a winemaker with the likes of Latour, Cheval Blanc and Haut Brion. These perfect winemakers in Bordeaux had been around for more than 300 years. Jonathan was an Englishman and a relatively new arrival in Saint-Émilion. He had cracked it: the 2015 vintage was awarded 95-96 points by the experts. It was simply nectar, especially aboard a little rowing boat in the Atlantic Ocean. Feeling slightly smashed I returned to row on into the night, the stars were shining bright and life felt pretty good. I also managed to fit in a few hours' sleep.

Day 12 and I sent a text to Simon with an opening line which read GMS (Good Morning Simon). Because everyone, everywhere seemed to be talking about everything these days using initials, I felt that I should too. He explained that his old laptop was on its final legs and all his data was being copied onto a shiny new one. He wouldn't have all the normal tools at his disposal today but I should just keep on carrying on. Having celebrated Australia Day only a few hours earlier, I replied 'no worries'.

Later that morning I received a text from 'the Midshipman', he was on good form and was just making contact for the first time. He wanted to let me know that he was now unable to concentrate on anything else in his life, he was mesmerised by the YB dots and my track over the ocean. I thanked him for his encouragement, I certainly needed it.

Today was the day on which one of my best mates was to have his memorial service. Sara would be going over to Sussex, to represent our whole family. I knew that I should have been there too. His death had been quite sudden in the November. But I felt that he would not have wished for me to have changed all the plans for the row. I also knew with his sense of humour and larger than life outlook on everything, he would have approved of my decision to just carry on out here. I didn't know then, but this was to be one of my most dangerous days at sea to date.

Everyone knows that in life, just when you think nothing else can possibly go wrong, it invariably does. The wind speed increased throughout the morning to around 22 knots from the East. The sea state at first light looked similar to a small mogul field. By lunchtime it resembled something akin to large houses, with waves smashing the transom and onto the aft solar panel. I had already had a quick stop for elevenses, a couple of Mars bars and more painkillers for my foot, all washed down with several litres of water. By early afternoon the seascape resembled those skyscrapers in Manhattan again, I knew I was in trouble. At precisely 15.40hrs while on the oars, the boat was hit on the port side by another enormous rogue wave, probably 40 foot high. The power of the water flipped the boat over like a toy rubber duck in the funfair. I wasn't attached by a harness and held on tight for my life to the grab lines just above my shoulders. It was a real surprise and a very weird feeling at the same time. The boat stopped rolling after a 170° rotation. Then slowly at first, she gradually righted herself and popped back up. I took a long deep breath of fresh air. I had survived my second knock down, this one in broad daylight, alive and well. Had the boat rolled through 360° this would have been classified as a full capsize, but that hadn't happened. I was drenched and the first thing I noticed was that my starboard oar had been snapped in half. I tried to pull myself together, nervous that another huge wave could slam into me at any moment.

I always ensured that all items on the deck were firmly secured with ropes and carabiners. Nothing appeared to have been lost overboard. I knew I shouldn't panic. Calmly grabbing my dagger board, I deployed this retractable board into a slot directly below the seat in the comms cabin. This immediately helped to stabilise the boat. The hydraulic arm, part of the autohelm, had detached from the rudder again. I switched to the hand steering ropes, then cleated them off at midships. I returned to the comms cabin to dry off.

As I reflected on what had just happened, I considered myself very lucky. Had I been attached to an uncomfortable 3-point safety harness. I might have easily ripped a hole in my stomach on the starboard oar gate as the boat went over. Worse still, have broken bones due to the force of the wave which had struck *Atlantic Rower*. I considered that maybe those safety ankle harnesses, with a much longer cord, might be safer during capsizes at sea. Before and after this experience I never wore my safety harness, except on a couple of occasions when I dived overboard to remove barnacles from the hull. I suspect I may be one of very few solo ocean rowers who have ever rowed an ocean completely detached from the boat. This is not sound advice for anyone else, I'm not proud of this, but it did work for me. I sent off a text to my meteorologist, explaining I was now one oar down with one spare to go. I also ensured that he knew that I wouldn't be telling Sara about this incident. He wisely suggested I should keep the oar parts; they might be useful at some point in the future if I broke another one. I poured myself another very large gin & tonic – I had survived another **critical incident**!

Later that evening the waves were still looking like mountains and the wind continued to blow at around 25 knots from the east. The boat was now riding through this in a more stable manner, largely thanks to the dagger board. I thought to myself, gosh what a day, it had started so calmly, it had turned rather nasty by lunchtime, I could have died by teatime. All the emergency procedures had been perfectly executed, by you know who (showing off to myself!).

A few minutes later my AIS alarm sounded. In the dark I couldn't see anything on the horizon so I stepped inside to check my chart plotter. It was 23.12 hrs. I was within 22 minutes of colliding with an enormous crude oil tanker called Mehle. She was sailing under a Panamanian flag, 274m long and 48m wide. She was coming straight at me, but she was so big and I was so small the skipper clearly hadn't seen me in the huge waves out here. I called him on the radio, I explained you've got to move now, because I have no motor nor sail. He changed direction at the very last minute. The waves were still so huge, I never even felt his bow wave as he passed near to my starboard side. After this heart stopper, I wondered why nobody had ever suggested that I could have had a radar reflector fitted to my mast. After all, these units are not expensive. With the benefit of hindsight, not having one of these was a big mistake – all ocean rowers in this day and age should have one. Despite all of this I was still wondering why this mother of an oil tanker hadn't spotted me on their AIS system. Had I not called them on my radio, they would have sunk me for sure.

This was to become 'The Longest Night', the fury of the ocean raged on all around me, and I had become completely disorientated. I had enormous difficulty trying to steer any course and I was expecting to be clobbered by another rogue wave at any moment. It was now after 23.30 hrs, I decided to call 'the Captain' (you will remember him from an earlier chapter, teaching me how to play with my chart plotter in the East Cowes marina). He and his charming wife were now sipping Killer Bees at Sunshine's Beach Bar & Grill on Pinney's beach, Nevis (as you do…). Initially when my Sat phone called his iPhone the normal prefix for a satellite phone appeared on his mobile. I discovered later that he felt this could be a Russian hooker, clearly calling an incorrect number. But his curiosity overcame him and he answered, hesitantly at first. The time there was around 18.30 hrs local time and just before dinner. What a life they were living, cruising around the Caribbean on their private yacht. Running water, hot showers, baths, a proper kitchen, fridge etc – how I longed for that sort of luxury. He quickly realised it was me on the other end of the call and we spoke for a good half an hour. He was always calm and made me laugh and this is what I needed right now. Having explained my predicament, he felt the best thing to do was to go as completely neutral as possible. Try to do sod all until first light. Stay in the relative safety of the comms cabin then try to steer a course of 235°. We hung up and I imagined him finishing off his Killer Bee rum punch. I tried briefly to steer a course as prescribed, but this didn't work. At first light I aimed for a course of 215° and this seemed to be just about possible given the current wild conditions.

An hour after I had hung up from 'the Captain', now around 00.15 hrs, I was still thinking of him sipping his Killer Bee punch on Nevis and felt I should have a drink to celebrate my survival through these extreme seas – after all, I had just had another **critical incident**. The large waves were still pounding the deck every couple of minutes. I reached for the Isle of Wight Mermaid Gin bottle but then remembered that the Fever-Tree tonic water was stowed in a food compartment, at the far end of the rowing deck. This was the furthest hatch away from the comms cabin. To get to the tonic water I would need to crawl along the deck, open the hatch and locate the mixer. I would then need to return to the comms cabin, without being thrown off the boat by an incoming wave and almost certainly be drowned. I also considered that if a big wave landed on the deck just as I had the hatch open, there was a sporting chance that the compartment would be flooded again with sea water. It was just too dangerous and I started thinking about improvisation. Did I have any other potential mixer with me in the comms cabin which could be a substitute for the tonic water?

I remembered that before the boat had been shipped from the UK, I had purchased a large tub of a powdered sports drink. This was loaded with electrolytes and flavoured with lemon and lime. I had been advised by a friendly neighbour that marathon runners and extreme athletes filled their water bottles with this. Diluted with water it gave them a nudge while out training. I thought to myself, why not give it a try. As they say in the disclaimers: 'Please don't try this at home!' I filled my glass with two large scoops of the powder, added water and topped it up with a triple Mermaid Gin. It was completely delicious even without ice; I was in heaven. After one sip it dawned on me that I had created a new cocktail, born at sea, to be called 'The Atlantic Mermaid'. I can strongly recommend it.

Day 13 and I decided before breakfast that if anyone wanted to take a cheap surfing holiday, then the East Atlantic was right up there with those waves featured in Hawaii 50. Why would anyone fly off to America when here it was on your doorstep? I had baked beans and sausages for breakfast mixed with several more max strength Ibuprofen tablets. My foot was still very swollen and painful, but I was fairly confident that no bones had been broken, just badly bruised.

Yesterday morning while I had been running the water maker, I had not switched the machine off correctly. For anyone not familiar with these machines, it is essential to only switch them off, just after the machine has made a loud 'clunk'. Because of the prevailing wave conditions at the time, I had just forgotten to do this. I knew that the main piston was now stuck in the middle of the barrel so it would not start up again, next time I switched it on. A year or so earlier I had driven over to Weston-super-Mare to participate in a professional water maker instruction course. This proved to be invaluable, I actually felt that I knew how to fix this problem. I opened the hatch in the comms cabin, methodically went through the process, screwing in the piston until it touched the end of the compression chamber and then unscrewing the bolt. To my complete surprise, when I flicked the switch to fire it up again, it worked perfectly. This was a massive relief; I knew that I wouldn't be dying from terminal dehydration any time soon. I ensured that both of my 10 litre jerry cans were filled to the brim – this acted as great ballast in raging seas.

Simon's new weather laptop was still being uploaded by his local IT shop. By 09.00 hrs, I've got an easterly wind now blowing directly behind the transom at about 18 knots and still very high seas. I made the decision today I would turn hard right. At last, me and my boat are now aiming at the Caribbean. I had mentioned to Simon that there was absolutely no sign of the butter melting. He asked if I was using Kerry Gold as that was calibrated for St Lucia. I replied that I was actually using Anchor butter from New Zealand, as with my navigational skills this might be a better option!

I would really put my back into it today, it was overcast and what else was there to do but row a bit harder. I had *Good Vibrations* from the Beach Boys playing at full volume on the deck; my mood was improving. I was also spurred on by one extraordinary thought. I knew that out here in the middle of the ocean, the closest I would ever be to another man or woman, was when the International Space station passed overhead. When that happened, it would be about 12 miles above my rowing boat! However, today was going to be very different: my granddaughter was flying with her parents to Barbados (very exciting for all of them). This meant that sometime this afternoon they would be flying above me, at around 7.5 miles above my head. I would try to wave at them if the cloud cover cleared and the skies turned blue…

Sunday morning, the weather forecast was for cloudy conditions but mostly dry and the wind had dropped to around eight knots from the east. This would be a good moment to catch up on a few chores. I checked all four deck hatches; three of them were still bone dry after my Gorilla taping. The largest of the forward hatches had a little water in it, but given the whole boat had been bombed by huge waves for days now, I felt this was a pretty good result.

I used fresh water to clear the salt crystals off both the solar panels with an extendable windscreen wiper. I replied to a couple of text messages from 'the Captain', then to 'the Midshipman' who had been texting to check if I was still alive. 'The Lieutenant's' wife sent a message explaining that the weather in England was cold, grey and drizzling. Everyone was looking fat and unhealthy, as was always the case at this time of the year.

I would call Sara this evening for a long chat and explain that I was absolutely fine and loving being out here. I've never been much good at doing my own washing. In fact, I had gone out of my way for the past 50 years, never attempting to turn on a washing machine. I could cope with the dishwasher but not the clothes machine. I knew that even trying to wash clothes on board a rowing boat was never going to be easy. I filled a bucket with fresh water from one of the jerry cans, lobbed in some Dr Bronners liquid soap and then added all my dirty clothes. I gave them a quick swirl around and got back on the oars, hoping that in a few hours' time they would be spotless.

Checking the bucket after lunch, I noticed that all my dirty clothes still looked dirty. I felt it best to leave them in there at least until tomorrow morning, when I would make another close inspection. I was in good spirits and rowed on until I was completely knackered that evening. After supper I called Sara and then collapsed in the sleeping compartment with the hand steering cleated off. Hoping I wouldn't be having any more of those close encounters with giant cargo ships, I slept like a baby; the previous week had clearly taken a toll on my body and I needed the rest.

EIGHT

The German Captain

I woke early on day 15 to learn that I was still the fastest rowboat in the East Atlantic…maybe I was the only one out here? Overcast with showers forecast for today and patchy wind. I replied to Simon: 'They never told me that the weather would be like this in the East Atlantic, had I known I would never have booked my holiday out here!'

Simon replied, 'Brochures always lie!'

At the end of his morning text, he added: 'Oh, and you need to bring the pedalo back in now.'

I was still laughing when I remembered my dirty clothes in the bucket on deck. My first chore was to check that they were now all bright and clean. They had certainly been tossed around for the past 24 hours in a similar manner to a washing machine. I looked into the blue bucket. None of the blood, sweat, grime, or spilt food had disappeared. I was confused; perhaps it was my choice of liquid soap or maybe something else. I knew right then and there I wouldn't be experimenting with my washing again on this outing. I would either row with just a hat and a pair of swimming trunks, or alternatively stark naked, which would probably be easier. I speculated that if a large ocean liner had pulled up alongside, this would not have been a pretty sight for the passengers. In desperation I wrung out the water from my dirty clothes and popped them into a large black plastic bin liner. Then unceremoniously dumped them into my new onboard rubbish bin. Out of sight out of mind, I thought to myself, I won't be needing those again!

During the day while making fresh water, the boat had been side swiped by another big wave, causing air to enter the water maker compression chamber. The incoming salt water pipe located in the hull had briefly been airborne. The machine immediately stopped. Only a couple of days ago, I had mastered the drill, moving the internal piston back into the correct position. To my relief it fired up again. I used the clean water today to fill a bucket which I left outside on the deck. I figured that when the sun was shining it would soon warm up the water and I would be able to indulge in a lovely hot shower. This worked a treat and was to become a regular event. It was a great way to wash and avoid salt sores for the rest of the trip. My blistered hands were also recovering by the day. I used the sawn-off finger rowing gloves whenever they were not completely drenched.

Having rowed all day non-stop, with a couple of brief pit stops for water and food, the light was going by 19.15 hrs. Soon after dark I was hit on the body by my first flying fish. Not a very big one, but a fish. This was to be the first of hundreds I would encounter and endure throughout the voyage. They just seemed to love the deck on *Atlantic Rower*. I rowed on throughout the night. During the early hours, I removed my dagger board as it was no longer required in these calmer conditions and it also caused the boat to slow down with the added friction under the hull, so better to lift it. I had a message from 'the Midshipman' yesterday, to watch out for Venus directly behind the boat as I would be dazzled by it. Unfortunately, it was a really cloudy night and I didn't get to see the stars at all. I did use the opportunity this morning as the weather was calmer, to make sure Uranus was in the right place. I now felt confident that I could move heaven and earth.

Tuesday morning loomed; sunshine was forecast for later today. I would have a chance to top up my meagre water supplies around midday when the sun was high in the sky. The boat had been blown north overnight after the wind had changed direction. Already this morning it was blowing at 12 knots from the ENE, it should be a good day on the oars. As I dictate this, a very large black cloud has appeared overhead. I'm excited, this may be one of those rare moments when I could take an early morning shower on the deck. In the event, the drizzle lasted for only 30 seconds, then it was gone and the sun was already appearing on the horizon behind me. No shower for me today.

I had decided on my second day at sea that I would not bother to shave during the voyage. It just seemed to be a complete waste of time when it could be better spent rowing. Never before in my life had I attempted to grow facial hair for more than a couple of days. It always just felt uncomfortable, but by today I was beginning to look a bit like Ernest Hemingway. That morning, I decided it was time to have another go at the mixed berry breakfast special. I have to confess it was delicious, but soon realised that most of it had become matted into my moustache or beard at every mouthful. Later in the day I would get the razor out and remove the lot. I rowed on, stopping for either a Kit-Kat, Mars Bar or Snickers whenever I felt in the mood, and sometimes just nuts. Drinking lots of water was a bit of a novelty for me – on land I usually preferred red wine. I had been spotted that afternoon by a couple of sea birds but still no fish, except the flying variety which by now covered the rowing deck most mornings.

At around 20.00 hrs, I received a text from my musical sister. It was a long message but the gist of it was her instruction: just to watch where I was going and be sure not to run into whales, destroyers or oil tankers. This may have been ESP (extra sensory perception) on her behalf, I only had to wait just over eight hours before my next **critical incident**.

I rowed into the night and stopped every couple of hours for a rest. Around 04.10 hrs, my AIS alarm sounded and woke me up. I reached over to the chart plotter to discover in the darkness that yet again I was in real danger of being run over. This time the ship coming straight at me was another huge crude oil tanker, much longer than the previous one, of a few days earlier. I grabbed the VHF and radioed on Channel 16: 'This is *Atlantic Rower*, OVER.'

The reply came back immediately from Captain Fredrik with a strong German accent, and the conversation went something like this:

'*Atlantic Rower,* this is Captain Fredrik speaking OVER.'

'Fredrik, thank heavens you picked up, you are on a collision course with my little rowing boat, *Atlantic Rower,* I don't have an engine, nor a sail, just two oars and I can't move out of your way, OVER.'

Still with a very strong German accent: 'You Ingleesh are so funny, I am standing on my bridge and I can't see any navigation lights, are they turned on? OVER.'

I immediately panicked; of course they were turned off, I was trying to conserve battery power. I replied to him:

'Hold on a minute, OVER.'

As I flicked the navigation light switch on, I could hear his voice booming down the radio:

'Ha, I can see you clearly now, OVER.'

'Captain Fredrik, my AIS is telling me that we will collide in about 17 minutes, could you please pass a message to your engine room, to turn hard to Port?'

The reply, with laughter came back: 'Vot do you mean, Pass the Port!?'

I replied, 'Captain Fredrik, this is no time to joke, time is running out, we will collide in about 16 minutes and counting, please steer to Port immediately.'

With an enormous sigh of relief, I could see the bow of the huge oil tanker moving to the left. I called Fredrik back and thanked him.

It was very soon after this incident that I worked out that I didn't really know my port from my starboard – it is confusing on a rowing boat sitting looking backwards! If I had got this wrong it would be all over now, I would have pegged it. I decided to write indelibly on the small whiteboard beside the VHF radio PORT = LEFT, this would avoid any possible confusion in the future. I poured myself another very large gin & tonic; this time it was easy to grab a Fever-Tree tonic from the aft deck compartment. Time stands still for no one at sea; having a proper drink at 04.30 hrs was becoming quite normal for me… So normal in fact, that my bar was beginning to run dry after so many **critical incidents**.

The following morning over breakfast and a nice cup of coffee, I considered again what had happened last night. It seemed to me that this was maybe the sixth time since I had departed from Gran Canaria, that I had picked up a potential incoming collision on my AIS system. However, none of these ships seemed to have picked me up on their AIS systems. I just couldn't understand this as I knew my AIS was working perfectly.

The forecast was for high cloud with some drizzle for day 17 at sea. I felt after everything I had been through recently, this sounded like the beginning of a calm day. My plan was to crack on SW, towards the Cape Verde Islands. It did turn out to be a calm day with lovely sunshine in the afternoon. I used the clothes pegs which Sara had packed for me, to start the drying out process of the borrowed hotel towel and other wet swimmers. I thought that one day I would go back to the hotel above the marina and return their towel. I had also packed a piece of sheepskin to be used on my rowing seat, should I develop a sore bum. Today was the initiation ceremony for this and it was very comfortable.

The oft-quoted narrative, that the Caribbean is 1,500,000 oar strokes away from Europe, doesn't hold much water with me. Maybe if you are some sort of super fit young body builder, making a living running marathons around the world. Running the 100m in under 10 seconds, this figure of 1.5 million oar strokes might be correct. But I'm just a normal chap, no one could ever describe me as an elite athlete, nor for that matter even an athlete. I'm not very fit and I was in my 68th year. I had no plans to completely attempt to change my physique for a bit of rowing. I never actually counted oar strokes. I do know that on my Concept 2 rowing machine back home in our garage, my average stroke rate was probably 25 per minute. After 30 minutes of this I normally felt completely and utterly shagged out and then collapsed. In fact, there were some days when I felt it was a miracle that I didn't actually have a stroke on the rowing machine.

Aboard *Atlantic Rower*, I was pulling well over a tonne of weight through the water and invariably my stroke rate slowed down. I'm guessing now that my average run rate might have been 18–20 strokes per minute. Call it 19 strokes and let's estimate that I'm actually spending 14 hours daily on the oars. Some days it was more and other days in storms, it would be less. I eventually rowed a total of 3,335 statute miles to get to Rodney Bay and it took me 72 days. In fact, this number of miles is surely an understatement of fact. The mileage figure is based on the four hourly YB tracker transmissions. I spent many days and weeks being blown off course, either in a north, south or easterly direction. These variations do not fully feature in a four hourly transmission tracker calculation (at least I don't think they do).

Using these basic parameters and not allowing for any course variation, then I would row a total of 1,150,000 oar strokes. This is clearly not the same as 1,500,000 strokes. As the crow flies, the distance from Gran Canaria to St Lucia is 140nm further than the distance from La Gomera to Antigua. If I had known this statistic before I set off, I would have considered starting my *sequel* in El Hierro, the most westerly island in the Canaries. For now, I was averaging about 16,000 oar strokes every 24 hour period. This would amount to just over 1,100,000 million oar strokes to St Lucia. This may sound like a lot and it is, especially if you are as unfit as myself…it's still a complete miracle that I ever got there!

I was now well and truly off Mauritania, still being visited on a regular basis by small gulls, one of whom seemed to be following me, but still no whales, dolphins or sharks. I concluded that my current latitude was still too far north to spot these potential visitors. Before supper I heard from 'the Midshipman'. He and his wife were off to try out the new 'Curry night' at a restaurant in Yarmouth. It would be many days before I heard from him again… Before signing off, I did mention that I had booked a table for one, with an ocean view, about 400nm due west of Mauritania!

Day 18 and the sea state reminded me of scrambled eggs again. My Garmin device was telling me that I had travelled exactly 1,000 statute miles. I couldn't remember if this also included the taxi ride from Portsmouth to Gatwick on the 3rd January, so I felt it wasn't the moment for another monumental celebration.

It was quite a relaxed 24 hours, the swelling in my left foot was at last subsiding, I was chewing my way through (another) large box of max strength Ibuprofen and it was having the desired effect. The best news all day had been a text telling me that our granddaughter had learnt how to crawl. She was still young and clearly a very fast learner. I felt this was most impressive. While rowing along, I had my first of many Walter Mitty moments.

What might she say to her guests later in life, entertaining friends as she approached her own 68th birthday? Would she remember what Grandpa had been doing at the same time all those years ago? Maybe she would ask her guests, 'You'll never be able to guess what my grandpa did when he was my age?' I was clearly beginning to lose it…

My musical sister had gifted me a small framed watercolour of a red squirrel before I departed from Blighty. This had been given to her many years earlier by our mother as an Easter present. It had been signed by both and was now hanging in the front nose cabin of *Atlantic Rower*. I would later sign this and gift it to our granddaughter, the red squirrel having been rowed all the way across the mighty Atlantic Ocean, with love from Grandpa.

I had several other Walter Mitty moments during the voyage. Many of these moments occurred while I was suffering from severe sleep deprivation. One of my most memorable daydreams happened on this very night. Anyone living today, who was born prior to the Coronation of Her Majesty Queen Elizabeth II, will remember that four days earlier Sir Edmund Hillary and Sherpa Tenzing Norgay reached the summit of Mt Everest on May 29th 1953. It was pure coincidence that these two great moments in history, happened at almost the same time. Both events were highly inspirational for the British people and Edmund Hillary was knighted soon after the expedition returned to England. In my daydream, I had this Walter Mitty moment – could I delay my transatlantic arrival so as to row solo into St Lucia just a few days prior to the Coronation of their Majesties King Charles III and Queen Camilla on Saturday 6th May 2023? If I could break the record then anything might happen! Dreaming is good for you; I have always believed everyone should dream a lot. If you really wish for something to happen enough, then you will make it happen. Time now to get back on the oars. Strange things happen after you've been at sea for 18 days with no other human contact.

Day 19, my weather text this Friday morning explained that I was still rowing mainly in the right direction. I had not been disturbed overnight by any colossal ships and all was well with the world. I was beginning to look a bit like a Mars Bar and my favourite Phil Collins' track, *One more night,* was playing on the deck. I had just enjoyed an apple with cinnamon breakfast, with an industrial strength coffee – what a great way to start any day. 'The Lieutenant' confirmed that I had rowed 874nm and that I only had 1,900nm to go. He said, 'Have a cigar on me, I'm sure there's a stub or two on board'. I explained that I was saving my only Monte Cristo No:2 for the Halfway line.

Yet again, the sea state resembled one of those unpleasant mogul fields in Val d'Isère. I had been given the heads up: more bad weather was coming my way soon. I knew I needed to pull my finger out and get further south before this weather hit. I spent some time in the middle of the afternoon, ensuring that everything which could move on the boat was secured properly, ahead of the impending storm. I then rowed as far as I physically could, through until first light on Saturday.

It was very wild all night and was still very wild the following morning, not gigantic waves but large waves and a growing swell. Overnight I had enjoyed an almost full moon again. These are really amazing out here, they helped me to see where my oars landed in the water, on every stroke. Four flying fish had landed and died on the deck during the night; I disposed of them in the sea. None of them had scored a direct hit on my body, but they were starting to smell as I threw them overboard.

Day 20 and the weekend again, I'm rowing with the quickest and most stable wave flow over the next couple of days. My meteorologist has signalled to me that the 'Big Stuff' is coming, stand by to stand by and all that. I had learnt by now that whenever he mentioned the 'Big Stuff' he wasn't joking. I hoped to row at least 48nm before 08.00 hrs tomorrow. One of my daily chores was to make a pencil mark on my small whiteboard in the comms cabin. Each vertical line represented another day at sea completed. After every five days I would use a diagonal line to join them up, like a tally mark you'd expect to find on a cell wall in Alcatraz. If I lost my mind before arriving on the other side, this record would be very useful for someone else!

Day 21, real excitement happened this afternoon at precisely 15.32 hrs. A pod of maybe 18 dolphins passed by my starboard side heading towards Africa. Instead of surfing these enormous waves with me heading west, they were headed in the opposite direction. In fact, they appeared to be airborne for most of the time as they dived up and through the oncoming waves. It was one of the most spectacular things I have ever seen in the wild. My camera was in the cabin. In these conditions I didn't dare get it out, in case it was completely drenched by an incoming wave. This moment, I have committed to memory forever. This was the first time I had seen a single fish since my departure (except for the flying variety) and this dolphin show was quite incredible.

In the past ten hours I had rowed just over 21nm, so I was on track to chalk up around 47nm before 08.00 hrs tomorrow. The only minor drama today was the appearance of a general cargo ship called Double Diamond, smaller than recent ships which had tried to wipe me out. She was only 177m long and 28m wide, she was flying a Marshall Island flag. I wondered whether she was full of beer and should I try to pull alongside? I radioed her skipper, he didn't speak much English, but we agreed there was never much risk of us having a prang. She eventually steamed past, at a distance of one nautical mile away from *Atlantic Rower*. If you're now beginning to think, wow it's busy out there in the Atlantic, you'd be right. I could hardly believe just how many large ships I had seen in such an enormous place, in such a short period of time.

That night, my autohelm became detached at around 03.51 hrs. This was due to a large wave breaking over the transom again. I was able to fix this after two attempts crawling around in the aft cabin. It wasn't broken and all is now well aboard the Good Ship Lollipop. I'm not sure where that name came from, but it seemed to roll off the tongue easier than *Atlantic Rower*, while recording this in my log.

Somewhere in the middle of the Atlantic Ocean, another visitor...

Storms off Africa

Tattered RVYC Ensign

Half way

NINE

Mission control

I've now completed three weeks at sea. It's 09.47 hrs, I'm hoping to have rowed exactly 1,000 nautical miles by high noon. I had almost forgotten just how crazy the sea was during the night. I was worried that the aft cabin would be buried in sea water every time I squeezed in trying to fix the autohelm in the dark. I had even considered being Captain Sensible (not normally something I'm very good at...) and wait for first light. I had rarely been sensible in my entire life – why should I start now?

As I continued rowing the sun rose higher in the sky. I noticed that my spanking brand new anemometer fitted just before departure by the best marine electrician in Cowes, had stopped working. This small item alone cost a small fortune and was a really useful weather instrument for any rower. Not only did it show exactly where the wind was coming from, but also accurately measured the wind speed. There were three small hard plastic hemispheres rotating just below the wind vane. I tried everything to get it working again but to no avail. I could only guess that seawater had entered the electronics after both of my recent knock downs. Both of these **critical incidents** had completely submerged the aft mast. As I rowed further south towards the Equator, the sun was getting hotter by the day. The salt water must have crystallized around the electronics inside the unit.

I was heartened by the fact that I was still flying the Royal Victoria Yacht Club Ensign. This helped me accurately guess wind direction and wind speed. In 1845 the club was granted a warrant to wear the Red Ensign of HM Fleet. From 1872-1898 the club held the warrant to wear the crown defaced Red Ensign. To this day members of the club can apply for a permit to wear this Ensign, as long as your boat meets certain criteria. The application is then approved on a five-year rolling basis. Before my adventure, I had been in real trouble for wearing said flag on *Atlantic Rower*, as well as on our 8.0m rigid inflatable boat. The woman in charge of flags had issued me a permit for our rigid inflatable boat some years earlier. I hadn't realised that I needed an individual permit for every boat we owned. I had screwed up again; there was nothing new about this. The club kindly suggested that I could also apply for a special permit for *Atlantic Rower*. I was very grateful; this special permit possibly saved my life while in the middle of the Atlantic. Even without my anemometer I was still able to have an idea of wind speed and direction, just by watching the Ensign. After this incident I read a lot more about flags in general. Flag etiquette is a mixture of law and maritime tradition. Not understanding correct etiquette could easily upset locals anywhere and everywhere. I'm now a world expert on the subject!

The wind speed had increased to about 30 knots from the NW, I was now suffering from severe sleep deprivation. I hoped to have a few naps during the day and a proper sleep that night. I spent some time trying to get good video footage of the mountainous seas using my very old GoPro 3. I wasn't able to play these sequences back on the boat, I would have to wait until I was on dry land for that treat. Sara messaged me around noon with the riveting news that I had now rowed 1,002 nautical miles in exactly three weeks and four hours.

At 14.03 hrs, while I was finishing off my lunch in the comms cabin, there was an almighty crash on the row deck. *Atlantic Rower* was hit by another gigantic wave and I failed to see it coming. It flooded the entire deck area, everything outside was awash with seawater for almost a full minute. Incredibly as the water flowed out through the gunwales, I could see that almost everything was basically intact. Only then did it become clear that I was missing my oar on the port side. My heart briefly stopped; on closer inspection the end of the oar had slipped out of the side holder. It was still attached to the row gate (rollock) by a flimsy piece of thin string and was now floating in the water. This had been another hairy experience; I would never again underestimate the power of the sea.

It was to become a long, wet and windy night with several dramas thrown in for good measure. All weather-related; the boat was battered all night long. There was no respite from the gale force winds, the seas remained enormous and the deck was flooded over and over again. I was completely drenched many times. I didn't get much sleep and had to visit the autohelm several times during the night. By now I had worked out that my autohelm only ever became disconnected after the boat had been given an absolute thrashing by a huge wave.

Day 23 at sea dawned, I kept myself together with the hope that today couldn't possibly be as bad as the previous one. The weather looked like it might drizzle all day and dark cumulonimbus clouds hovered above my head. I concluded that rowing in broad daylight was much easier than spending all night on the oars. But in wild weather, I couldn't ever afford to sleep for more than 20 minutes at a time.

From my audio log: 'It looked more and more like I might get a proper rain storm sometime today. If it doesn't happen then at least it's forecast for later this week. Either way if I get the chance to strip off and have a proper shower, I should be less smelly by the weekend. It happened at 14.29 hrs and it was just wonderful. I'm now drying off and watching the sea at the same time. The waves are still absolutely gigantic and the wind is blowing behind the boat at about 28 knots from the ENE. This would continue for most of tonight. Still no whales but I enjoyed supper with another serving of salmon and a warm tin of Foster's lager from Melbourne. I had been starboard side on to the waves, for much of the night and can't really explain how I felt at first light.'

I was completely exhausted and wondered if this introduction to the Atlantic would ever come to an end. Surely there would be days on the ocean when I could just relax and soak up a few rays, without spending hours contemplating another full or partial capsize.

Day 24 and I've just sent Sara, head of mission control in Fishbourne, an update. How on earth was she always able to get my clothes so clean, this was still a complete mystery to me. I had just hung a T-shirt out to dry on the starboard grab line, and it still looked as though it had been worn by a coal miner!

It was a sunny morning, my prayers had been answered, I planned to dive overboard in the coming days to attempt to clean the barnacles off the hull. The boat had now been in the water for almost 38 days, including two weeks at the marina. I could almost feel the drag caused by algae and barnacles creating friction. Pulling the oars through the water, my rowing speed had dropped by about half a knot.

The sunshine didn't last long. By early afternoon I was clobbered by an Atlantic squall which literally came out of nowhere (they always do!). Fifty knot winds from every direction and huge seas, but I managed to fit in another proper shower. It was all over almost as soon as it had started; sunshine then replaced the gloom. It took me a while to ensure that I was rowing again in the right direction. Everything becomes very disorientated in a squall, to the point where I hadn't got a clue which way was north or south for several minutes. The main compass on the aft bulkhead didn't ever help me much, due to the fact that the view from the rowing seat was inversed. 'The Captain' had explained to me how useless it was, back in the East Cowes marina. Given the compass was facing backwards and set to magnetic North, I would be best to ignore it completely. I soon realised that I was fine and the boat was fine, so spent a bit of time doing daily chores. Ensuring my rubbish was properly stored, the solar panels sparkling, the deck clear of flying fish and generally washed down with clean water. It's much easier to row any boat if it's clean and well organised. I was now ready for the next drama on the high seas.

That evening, I switched on an audiobook entitled 'A promised Land' written and orated by Barack Obama. I loved the man, he himself talking me through the story of his time in high office. This was the first time I had ever listened to an audiobook and it was a 29-hour recording. I hoped that I may get through it all before I arrived on a sunny beach in the Caribbean Sea. The sunny beach moment was still well over 2,000 statute miles away, so actually finishing his story was not going to be a big problem. I rowed on into the night, was hit in the face by a large flying fish, but managed to get in a few solid hours' sleep. No close shaves with other boats and awoke to discover I had only rowed 35nm in the past 24 hours.

First light on Thursday, my plans to dive in were scotched by the sight of another wild morning. I had been warned to be careful cleaning the hull. If the boat was broadsided by a large wave while I was underwater, I could easily be knocked unconscious. For this reason, I had purchased a very smart yellow crash hat. If the boat did land on top of me, I should be fine. These hats are normally worn by whitewater canoeists to avoid being decapitated on rocks.

I stopped for breakfast and as I opened the ration bag another note dropped out. It read: 'Come home soon! The rubbish needs taking out! I need you!'

I expected another relatively low mileage day, which was fine. I plugged away, slapping on some suncream to my forehead, nose and lips, all of which had already been burnt to a cinder. The sun/

wind effect and being surrounded by water magnified the harmful rays of the sun. I rowed on throughout the day, occasionally stopping for water, chocolate bars or nuts and eventually supper. I had found it harder to pull the boat through the water today. I put this down to the barnacles, all the time hoping I might be able to take the plunge first thing tomorrow morning.

'The Captain' made contact. He and his wife had been so supportive ever since I had purchased *Atlantic Rower*. They were checking in on my mental and physical state. I replied that I was mentally fine, at least I didn't think I had gone loopy yet (they all say that!). I asked 'the Captain' if he had been able to get me that reservation at the local Loonie bin in St Lucia for my arrival? He laughed and I explained that physically I had never felt better. Before we hung up, I explained to him that while I was now technically enjoying the Trade winds, they felt more like the Doldrums.

Friday morning, the sea state was calm and the moment had arrived. Before diving in, I called up and double checked with Duncan. He didn't actually offer me any advice, but as I explained to him exactly how I planned to do this, he nodded his approval over the phone. I had never practised this exercise until now in the mid–Atlantic. I turned the boat sideways onto the incoming waves, cleated the rudder off using the hand steering ropes and attached the rope ladder to the port side of the boat. I figured that if a shark or some other deadly fish decided to have a go at me, then at least I should be able to get back on the deck as quickly as possible. I also removed the rowing foot rests and had a bucket full of water at the ready. This would be useful to remove the salt from my body once back on deck. As I dived overboard, my first thought was that I should have done this sooner. The water was cool, this was the first time in well over three and a half weeks that I was able to have a proper wash. I decided not to look around for sharks; the water was almost 12,000 foot deep below me. For the first and penultimate time in my voyage, I was attached by my 3-point safety harness to the boat. I fastened to this, a couple of extra six foot safety lines with carabiners. This would enable me to swim around the hull, without the need to get out at half time and change sides. The hull was completely covered in algae and barnacles. I tried to remove these with a large white 3M scratch pad but this had absolutely no effect at all. I decided to get out and find the plastic windscreen ice remover. I had thrown this somewhere into the back of the boat, just for good measure before my departure.

Back in the water and still no sign of any sharks or Portuguese men of war jellies, I spent almost an hour with a snorkel trying to scrape off as much as possible. During the process I inhaled a lot of seawater. When I eventually got out and leant forward on the deck, the best part of half a pint of seawater poured out of my nose. My body was frozen and the prevailing wind didn't help either. I wrapped myself in towels and warmed up, then made a nice cup of coffee to warm me inside. I had survived this episode without incident. I realised that there was still more to be done on the centre line, but that would have to wait for another day. My smart yellow canoe helmet was still brand new; I hadn't needed it. Towards the end of the dive while removing barnacles from the rudder, I had been clobbered a couple of times but I hadn't drawn blood. While underwater I had seen a multitude of small fish feeding off the bottom of my hull. I was not alone out here!

During the afternoon I noticed seaweed floating on the water beside the boat. I didn't know then, but was to discover later that this stuff was called Sargassum. This was to become a big problem later in the crossing as it frequently got caught on my rudder. Worse still, it would almost completely block the pre-filter chamber on my water maker. This seaweed had originally been beneficial to the marine ecosystem, but had been spreading dangerously since 2011 due to human pollution. Later that evening I enjoyed a spectacular shooting star show, which made for great entertainment.

As the new day dawns, I'm rowing faster with my near spotless hull. I've been advised by text that I'm now between two big weather bands, one to the north and one just to the south. I should expect lightning from the latter. Having not encountered thunder and lightning, even once since I departed, this was going to be something of a novelty. I remembered the song from Bohemian Rhapsody, *Thunderbolt and lightning, very, very frightening.* I certainly didn't want to be struck down out here. Light winds forecast for today and over the weekend but picking up next week.

Later that afternoon I realised that I was on a collision course with another large cargo ship called Topeka, 295m long and 46m wide, travelling in my direction at 11.6 knots. I had a long chat with them on the radio; they were very friendly. I asked the skipper to please move out of my way and he obliged. The highlight for me today was calling up and speaking to all of my direct family for the best part of an hour. They were all on the Isle of Wight for the weekend and I was missing them. I knew that there was absolutely nothing I could do about this while stuck out here in the middle of an ocean. Hearing from them all, really made me wonder again, what on earth was I doing. That said, during my entire voyage, I never had time to feel alone or lonely. There was always just too much going on to spend time looking inward.

The conditions were no longer conducive to rowing; the sea was calm, the wind had dropped and I didn't even get hit by that electrical storm. Rowing through treacle, the final excitement for the day was the approach of yet another ship on almost exactly the same path as Topeka, called Frederica. She was sailing under the flag of the Bahamas, a mere 186m long and 28m wide. Similar to Topeka, they told me that I was not showing up on their AIS system, even though they were very clearly showing up on mine. I decided that both of these skippers must have been asleep at the wheel. I thought the problem was just that my little boat was hidden by the huge swell and the waves. I brushed this off as not being a problem. It was exciting to see big ships sailing by in daylight – most of my previous encounters had been in the darkness of night. Today was the first day when I discovered I was able to take screen shots on my chart plotter. This would prove very useful much later, when I eventually wrote this book. I sent a text to 'the Captain', just mentioning all these near collisions. He replied, suggesting I should ask someone to confirm that my AIS was transmitting. By the time I had my next near miss I had completely forgotten to heed this advice, so I was still none the wiser for some considerable time to come.

Sunday 12th February dawned, this was my 28th day at sea, so I felt the 28 nautical miles rowed yesterday was a very appropriate number. Simon's text indicated that Monday and Tuesday looked better and the wind should increase from almost zero to about 18 knots from the ENE. Apart from a couple of squalls during the night, the sun was now shining and it was going to be a good day.

Before I departed, I always felt there was a sporting chance I might be blown north from the Canary Islands and end up in a bar in Casablanca. Bob Hope had always been one of my heroes. I had loved watching the Road to Morocco in black and white, starring Bob, Bing Crosby and Dorothy Lamour. By complete chance, the moment when I could have been washed up on the shores of Morocco had now passed. Sara and I agreed, that given my current position, today would be a good moment to tell a few more friends about my adventure. So long as I was able to resist the temptation to stop off at the Cape Verde Islands and rent a deckchair, they could watch any future progress on my YB tracker. The chances now of my being shipwrecked anywhere along the coast of West Africa were at best unlikely. Many of these friends had already given very generously to the charity and now more donations rolled in. Every time I was told that someone had made a donation it made me happy; it was also a great incentive for me to row harder and try to get to the other side sooner.

Later that morning, I tried again to do a bit of washing. This time I put two table cloths in the blue bucket, added at least half a bottle of Dr Bronner's liquid soap and some fresh water. Finally, I stirred everything around with a long bamboo back scratcher. After 30 minutes I rinsed them in cold water and using the clothes pegs, hung them out to dry on the grab lines. Initially they do look quite clean, well actually not that clean. That would be almost the last time I tried to wash anything on this trip… What on earth was I doing wrong, even when I thought they were quite clean, I must have been hallucinating.

I had discovered that in between some rather unpleasant meals, I had packed a large quantity of McVitie's Ginger Nut biscuits. The packets which had survived the flooding weeks earlier, were absolutely delicious. I rationed myself to two biscuits a day and they became enormous treats. I rowed on through the night, watching shooting stars, and only dropped the oars on the water occasionally for coffee and Mars bars. When I was completely shattered, tired and exhausted I would stop for a couple of hours' sleep. The last four weeks had taken their toll. I hoped from now on, my passage might be slightly calmer to enable more down time.

During the night there must have been a flash of lightning, not a full blown lightning strike, but sufficient to affect most of my electronic stuff. I reset various items and all now seems to be well again. Then at 05.48 hrs, I picked out the lights of another ship on the horizon. Checking my chart plotter, she was called HP Stella, she is about 5nm to my port side. A minnow at 160m long, compared with some of the gigantic super tankers which I've been avoiding. I didn't call them up on the radio, because we're not going to have a collision (phew!).

TEN

Halfway

The so called 'Trade winds' have yet to fully reveal themselves and it's day 29 at sea. By now the butter had well and truly melted (all over the deck). I was in calmer water, there was no proper wind direction and there was another cyclone forming well north of my position later this week. I was warned that this was likely to stuff the Trades again. The nights were certainly getting warmer and I decided the time had come to bin my sleeping bag. This by now was quite whiffy and damp from the condensation in the sleeping cabin. I rolled it up into a black bin liner and ejected it into my onboard dustbin (the front food deck hatch). I never needed it again. It wouldn't be very long now before I was running a small electric desk fan in the comms cabin, to keep me cool, especially in the middle of the day.

I made contact with the Castle Road gang and the High Street crew in Cowes. They had been avid supporters of this adventure from the outset. They just loved the idea of an old bloke doing something silly. A great friend from Castle Road kept the others fully in the loop throughout the voyage. Sara and I would have a huge lunch with most of them on our return, at the Island Sailing Club.

I received a text message this morning telling me that I would almost certainly overtake some of the 2022 Challenge rowing boats before I arrived in the Caribbean. I dismissed this text as complete nonsense. I did know that they had departed from La Gomera on schedule on Monday 12th December 2022. I had departed exactly five weeks or 35 days after them, on Monday 16th January 2023 from an island further away from their departure point and my final destination. I certainly wasn't in a race with these rowers, but concluded there was a zero chance that I would be overtaking any of them ever.

For the first time in many weeks, I had a fairly normal day on the oars. I played a lot of music through my deck speaker, still paired to my iPhone. *Take it easy,* by The Eagles, *One more night,* by Phil Collins, *I'll find my way home,* by Jon & Vangelis, and many other tracks. I really enjoyed *Made in England,* hammered out by Elton John. Quite often I sang along to the music, trying to kid myself that I hadn't gone crazy, at least not yet. The clean hull certainly made a difference. If I had realised this earlier, then I would have jumped overboard to clean it sooner. But the weather conditions had never allowed for this during the early part of my row.

I was to discover much later that a four-man independent rowing boat, named 'Team Bahrain mission Atlantic', had departed from Pasito Blanco in Gran Canaria on 23rd December 2022. This was just down the coast and only about 25 miles from the Puerto Rico marina. Four days into their row, the boat named ORB Endurance had capsized in very high seas. Fortunately, the four-man crew had all been safely rescued by chopper. The boat was still afloat after they had been rescued. The unmanned boat was eventually spotted by a tourist aboard the Disney Cruise ship 'Fantasy', 250nm north of Hispaniola in the Caribbean Sea. I mention this because ORB Endurance had drifted with the Trade winds and the currents for more than 260 days. She had eventually arrived relatively near her planned destination, which had been Barbados. These boats are very well constructed. This is not something you necessarily believe, especially when you are out in the middle of an ocean for the very first time. It has been speculated, that if you tried to cross an ocean without rowing at all, then you would eventually arrive somewhere near your destination. This is clearly correct; however, you would be stone dead, long before reaching halfway. Standard rations, even for a solo rower, only allow for 84 days at sea, not 260 days!

I knew I had rowed far enough south; I now needed to row west. Given the adverse wind direction, I found this very difficult and started to worry that I might end up somewhere in South America. I'm now well over a thousand miles from anywhere, there is no light pollution, just beautiful clean air to breathe, and extraordinary night time skies.

Today is St Valentine's Day. Since we were married, and well before then, I've never missed one of these. I just hoped that Sara was happy and would call her later for a long chat, sending my love from the ocean. Prior to my departure I had organised with my youngest daughter for a Valentine's Day card to be sent home. This should have arrived on the day in my own hand writing, making a nice surprise.

Then just when I thought nothing else could possibly go wrong, my music abruptly stopped playing. Inspecting my iPhone, not only had it stopped playing, but it was all being deleted, track by track. I thought I had downloaded everything several months earlier so this was really strange. I wasn't even at the halfway line, so it was a complete mystery to me and a complete disaster at the same time. Prior to donating most of our old CDs to a charity, we had made an effort to save the best music. We had downloaded them onto our first generation, Brennan music player. These songs, maybe 250 of them, I had copied onto my iPhone. They were all still available on a downloaded playlist. However, the best music which I thought I had downloaded using the Shazam app, was also all being deleted as I watched. Originally, when adding these songs to a playlist, I thought I had more than 750 tracks. It took my youngest daughter about five minutes to work out that I had added several of the same tracks, multiple times. For example, there were 27 copies of *My way*, by Frank Sinatra!

I sent a text to Sara. 'Come in Fishbourne, we have a problem'. This was one of those rare moments during the voyage, when I felt I should directly trouble her with one of my problems at sea. I had lost most of my music. She replied almost immediately that, clearly, I hadn't downloaded it correctly and because I had been out of internet range for just over four weeks now, the music would only return when I was back on land and connected! The moral of this story for all future ocean rowers: make sure the music is actually downloaded properly, before you try to row the Atlantic Ocean!

I've rowed just over 18nm today since 08.00 hrs, it's now 17.00 hrs, so the total should be over 40nm by tomorrow morning. If I was to have another 70nm day, then I would be delirious, but it's not going to be today. I figured that I couldn't be that far away now from the halfway line, especially if those phantom Trade winds decided to start blowing from the east. Later that evening I settled down to another delicious supper and a tin of Heineken. Foolishly, I had only packed six tins – what on earth must I have been thinking when I provisioned the boat? I am not even half way to St Lucia. The entire contents of my bar aboard *Atlantic Rower* now consisted of two tins of Heineken, two nips of Mermaid Gin and two cans of Fever-Tree tonic water. I also had one bottle of 2015 Chateau Gloria, a gift from our son. This was only to be opened in the event of an emergency or when I actually made it to the halfway line. The following morning loomed, the blisters on both my hands had largely recovered, helped by the rowing gloves, the swelling in my left foot had completely subsided and apart from a few cuts and bruises, I was in good shape.

How the days seem to all blend into one out here. It's breakfast time again and the moment has come to try a wet packet of scrambled eggs with bacon and baked beans. This didn't taste half as good as the same thing at your normal greasy Joe café. In the same ration bag, I found another piece of handwritten paper which read: 'Save the neck for me, Clark' – Cousin Eddie. I was a huge fan of all the National Lampoon's movies. Chevy Chase for me rates as one of the funniest actors in history. This made me smile and as I downed my scrambled eggs, I watched the sun appear over the horizon from the direction of Africa.

Simon seemed even more excited than myself, with his comment 'lovely course and faster – yay!'. He forecast a sunny day, winds from the east 15-20 knots and proper Trade winds at last. But the outlook for the coming days was miserable, the low-pressure cell to the north would suck out anything that was left of the Trades later this week. I decided to go for it, I rowed my socks off (even though I never wore a pair of socks for a single day during the voyage). With the help of a lot of chocolate bars and several Snickers, I would row just over 53nm on my 30th day at sea.

Day 31 and my meteorologist's early morning text explained the outlook for the coming weekend was for unsteady, messy, patchy winds and currents. This was not something that I wanted to read. I asked him if I should get my para-anchor ready on the deck, and he replied hopefully not.

I had been texting and speaking to 'the Captain'. He was back aboard his yacht and now sailing towards Martinique. He was keen to hear again, how was I feeling physically and how was I feeling mentally. I replied by text. You know, I'm feeling absolutely fine but thanks very much for asking. I remember wondering if 'the Captain' ever thought I was being serious. He had been simply brilliant both before and during my voyage. While I had originally awarded him the rank of 'the Captain', it wouldn't be long before he received a major promotion…

'The Lieutenant' was going to give me the heads up when I got close to the halfway signpost in the middle of the Atlantic, just in case I happened to miss it. His role throughout the voyage was to be as important as that of 'the Captain'. To date he had been incredibly generous with his massive support for the charity and his constant humour. 'The Lieutenant' and the Red Baron, were joint cheer leaders for this important cause. The difference both had already made to the fundraising total was way beyond my wildest dreams. All of this was very important to me; after all, I was on a mission to help save the red squirrels from extinction on the Isle of Wight.

I was also receiving daily text messages from 'the Midshipman'; these were always very positive and encouraging. But there was often more content regarding the newly laid lawns at home. Last autumn he had sprayed them all with a massive overdose of weedkiller, mistaking it for fertiliser. I felt I was the only person alive who could easily have bungled on that scale! The state of the ocean in which I was only just surviving was the least of his worries right now.

Halfway. I registered 037° N, 20° W at 17.33 hrs on the 14th February. 'The Lieutenant' supplied this information. My confidence in his maths had always been unwavering. He also understood how to calculate a P/E ratio, something which I had never understood during my entire working life. It had taken me slightly less than 31 days to row to the middle of the Atlantic Ocean. As I rowed past this important milestone, I could feel a slight downhill gradient. I laughed and laughed, it's all going to be downhill from now on. 'The Lieutenant's' coordinates had been perfect. My odometer also told me the same: I have covered 1,752 statute miles so far, plus or minus the taxi ride from Portsmouth to Gatwick before departure. That's enough statistics from me today.

I decided the moment had come to open the 2015 vintage Chateau Gloria. I had forgotten to pack a decanter, but I raised my glass to the heavens and toasted my son for giving me this superb bottle. I had cooked up a delicious very late lunch, of avocado with chilli, to be followed by a Jimmy's iced coffee. This should all go well with the claret. Before eating, I was so excited that I went into the comms cabin and took a screenshot at precisely 037° N, 20° W to show the position of *Atlantic Rower* in the Ocean. I then took another photo of the opened bottle of Chateau Gloria. It was only much later when the adventure was over, that I ensured our son was able to forward these pictures to the owners of the Chateau in St Julien. I attached a caption, 'You can drink Chateau Gloria Anytime, Anyplace, Anywhere on Planet Earth'. They thought this was pretty cool, posting it on their social media pages which created literally hundreds of 'likes'! The owners of the Chateau then completely surprised me when I returned home a few months later. They delivered a signed DB (double magnum) of the same wine, in an old wooden case, specially engraved '**ATLANTIC ROWER**'. I will treasure this and it will only be opened when we celebrate the next very special occasion. Great wine and great people – what more could anybody ask for in life?

I received a reply to my message from our son: Hope it's not corked, remember to take a photo, so happy for you, well done. You know who, sends her love too.

More rowing, more music including *Cecilia* from Simon & Garfunkel and *Surfin USA* by the Beach Boys. Thank heavens I still had the 250 soundtracks from my old Brennan playlist, properly downloaded and available. Lovely clear skies and zero pollution, more Kit-Kats and more sweat, more heat, more rays and about to be more flying fish, as darkness descends after a good day on the oars. I should just mention here that the daytime temperature is now significantly higher than when I was in Gran Canaria. In fact, it is bordering on being really hot. At around 04.00 hrs, the temperature inside the sleeping cabin is still 31° Celsius and the relative humidity around 88%. I'm still sticking to UTC, with no time correction for my passage westwards. This means that the sun is rising later every morning. To put this into context, here we are on Wednesday 15th February and the sun is coming up over the horizon at 08.45 hrs.

It's an overcast day with black clouds around the boat and the winds have dropped, it's now blowing from the ENE at around eight knots. Simon's daily weather forecasts were so accurate, I often wondered if he was actually following me in a boat just a few miles away. Today I felt that I should ask him the question directly. Was that him in the small white boat just over the horizon? He replied, assuring me that he was still working from home, operating his meteorological magic from a garden shed, in the south of England.

Waves are now coming at me from every direction. Today is my younger brother's birthday and he loved my rendition of *Happy Birthday* sung over the satellite phone from the middle of the ocean. I thought we might never stop chatting. After the call I managed to down another one of those delicious Alaskan salmon lunches. Later that evening I made a couple more calls to friends and family just to give them an update. I was only disappointed not to have spotted the halfway signpost and bewildered that I still hadn't seen any whales or sharks.

I stopped rowing around 01.15 hrs, needing some sleep. I was tired but the excitement of being on the second half of my journey hadn't been lost on me. After the best part of an hour, I awoke to the loud sound of grating directly below where I was snoozing. I knew that the ocean here was at least four miles deep, there was no way I could have got snagged on a reef or anything similar. The noise came and went and then returned. It had to be a shark, how large I had no idea; maybe it was just plain curious or maybe it was trying to rub something off its body. I'll never know, but I was mighty glad when the noise eventually stopped and I was able to get back to sleep.

Having rowed on and off overnight, it's now Friday morning, my 33rd day on the Atlantic. I should expect an overcast day with some showers, ENE winds around 12 knots with a very patchy forecast for the coming weekend. It was very difficult to row in a straight line in these conditions. I had enjoyed a beautiful partial moon last night with a stunning night sky.

I had asked Simon this morning if he thought I would get the opportunity to sight whales in this part of the Atlantic. He replied, probably not as the water may be too warm now. I was so disappointed by this – one of the reasons for this row had been the hope of seeing whales close up.

So far, I hadn't even been able to imagine one of them. This was all about to change big time. What was about to happen would overshadow some of those great safari moments in East African game reserves. Normally in that situation, one is strapped into a land cruiser or something similar. You are told not to put your hands out of the window and the stunning wildlife sometimes sniffs around your motorised vehicle. The park ranger gives you the heads up well in advance if you might just be about to see something very special. Well out here, you're not strapped in (at least I wasn't), you are only 18 inches above the water and you get absolutely no advance notice from the park ranger. On an ocean most people tend to go out on tourist boats to go whale watching at huge expense. What was about to happen was fundamentally the complete opposite. The whales were about to come and watch me, in my little boat…

The time was around 16.00 hrs, I was rowing towards the Caribbean, minding my own business in calm seas; my music was turned off. I always charged the Fusion speaker battery during the height of the day, while the sun was fully overhead. I was looking about 150m behind the boat. I could see what looked like the hull of a very large upturned superyacht without a keel. I decided it was so huge that it would be a serious danger to shipping even out here. I had better call the US Coastguard. As I turned to grab my satellite phone from the comms cabin, I had one final look and noticed that it was moving around in front of my eyes... It was one enormous whale sunbathing on top of the water! Worse still, I must have rowed right over the top of it, just before it had come up for air. This was a complete disaster, no photographic evidence, nobody would ever believe me! I dropped the Sat phone and grabbed my iPhone with the built-in camera. I had only ever taken this out on deck in very calm conditions. I had always worried that if it got knocked by a wave or if I dropped it into the water, I would be in dire straits. It had my remaining music stored on it and it was my keypad for sending Garmin Sat text messages. It also had all my photographs from earlier in the row. None were backed up due to no internet and I was still about 1,500 miles away from any land mass. By the time I held the camera pointing at the whale it was all too late. I could still just about see him or her with the naked eye, but there was no way I could get a photograph, just too far away now. I was distraught – throughout my entire voyage the one thing I had really wanted to see, were whales in their own habitat.

I didn't have to wait very long for this dream to come true... Within five minutes I was back on the oars. To the starboard side of the boat, from the blind side, two metres away from where I was sitting, up came the head of an enormous sperm whale. I completely froze. Very slowly I placed the oars gently on the water, I turned to grab the iPhone and as I looked again, a second equally enormous whale came up for air just behind the first one. This was followed soon after by a third whale, about 20m away from the boat. I madly started snapping the camera. It's fair to say I was in a complete state of shock, a bit like a rabbit caught in the headlights. The first whale beside the boat was within touching distance. We eyeballed each other and I soon realised that these amazing creatures were not going to harm me. They had just surfaced because they had heard the unusual sound of my oars in the water. They would have been used to the thud of a large ship's propellor or the noise from an engine room.

What I didn't know at that time, was that sperm whales grow to be 67 foot long and weigh in at around 45 tonnes. They are the third biggest whales on the planet after the blue and fin whales. Sperm whales are the world's largest predator. Their teeth are between 4-8 inches in length. If one of them had swum under my boat and then surfaced, it would almost certainly have been all over. The two whales nearest to me seemed to be playing, and had just come up to see what the fuss was all about. I continued for maybe ten minutes taking photographs of them all. They were still very close to *Atlantic Rower* and I did consider again, what happens if one of them decides to swim underneath my hull. They were completely happy, even giving me a few 45° blasts from their blow holes. Eventually, when I was exhausted from the excitement, one at a time they performed the most perfect dives, their tails, known as flukes, high in the air. These flukes look very similar to the tee tail of a Boeing VC10. They were gone as quickly as they had arrived. I took more film of this. When I made land, I sent some of my pictures to the Whale Foundation and The National History Museum. I needed to check that they actually were sperm whales. They acknowledged this and congratulated me on some extraordinary photographs. Perhaps they were most extraordinary because my rowing seat was so close to the water line. These whales had not only made my day but they had also made my adventure; I was still completely speechless. I can't put into words just how gigantic they actually are, especially when compared to the length of my little boat. I felt very humbled and honoured that they had taken time out to come alongside and say 'Hello'.

My AIS system warned me of another cargo vessel in the vicinity called Stella Navas, but I completely ignored them as the whale show was still in the forefront of my mind.

I had been suffering from a strange feeling over the past couple of weeks. When lying down after long sessions on the oars, it felt as though I was falling into an abyss. This feeling lasted for no more than 30 seconds. It was slightly unnerving and it was happening more and more often. I'll never know for sure what caused this. It could have been blood rushing to my head when I was laid out or it could have been related to sunstroke and dehydration; it was certainly very unsettling.

Day 34, the good news today was that my weather forecaster felt I was bang on course. I should hit the correct Caribbean Island (St Lucia) in about another 1,500 miles. The bad news was that I was due to have the equivalent of a wet weekend in Bognor. The wind was almost non-existent with an occasional puff from the SE at five knots. It felt like I was rowing through very thick treacle, this would slow me right down to a snail's pace.

The calm sea was a perfect environment for me to see through the beautiful clear blue water under the boat. Today would be the first time when I saw a large, bright turquoise fish swimming under the hull. I had no idea what it was except her colouring was completely spectacular. I was excited by this and when she returned later in the afternoon, even more excited.

I decided that in these conditions, it was a good moment to listen to a bit more of Barack Obama. After all, there was little other sound around, and it felt like there was zero chance of a rogue wave knocking me for six today. I was feeling absolutely great, I knew I was now on the second half of my adventure. I reflected on the whale show yesterday and decided that I had been very lucky indeed to have seen them at all. They normally tend to travel further north at this time of the year to be in cooler waters. I concluded that my visit from the whales had been an absolute fluke (excuse the pun). Nightfall was now happening later and later every day – this evening it would only get dark after 21.10 hrs.

Someone had told me before I set off, that the Isle of Wight is closer to the North Pole, than the distance I would have to row to get across the Atlantic Ocean. In the final event it would be an extra 620 miles on top of that to St Lucia.

Sunday 19th February, yesterday was my slowest day since I started out, 24nm was embarrassingly slow. I knew that anyone watching my YB tracking device might assume that *Atlantic Rower* had been holed under the water line. The text from my meteorologist around 09.00 hrs confirmed my worst fears. These weather conditions were here to stay, today and for the entire new week ahead. The muddled winds were blowing the boat from different directions at around eight knots. I could see Atlantic squalls forming on the distant horizon. An Atlantic squall is something to behold. With very little notice a huge cumulonimbus cloud with a very dark bottom, would literally park itself directly above the boat. It then starts to rain heavily, followed by winds which come at you from every direction. Squalls always left me feeling completely unnerved. They would normally only last for 15 minutes but this was sufficient to seriously disorientate me. Once one of these had passed over *Atlantic Rower*, then there would be a long period of calm. This was because any wind left behind in the vicinity of the squall, would be sucked up into it as it grew in intensity. Probably a bit like a tornado.

My children had given me a really smart Sony Walkman headset, so I had a back-up of all the music which had originally been saved on our old Brennan. I wondered if I had remembered to copy some of the Shazam tracks over to this amazing headset. I tested it out and while all the downloaded tracks were still available, none of the iTunes nor the Shazam tracks were on this device. Never mind, this gadget had already been completely brilliant throughout the force 10 gales and storms earlier in my voyage. My Fusion speaker on deck wouldn't have lasted more than five minutes in those conditions.

Today became the first day and the first night out here, when the wind had blown around the clock from either the south or the west. This had made it virtually impossible to row forward, without immediately being blown back towards Africa. This now happened every time I stopped for water or a meal or just a snooze. McVitie's Ginger Nut biscuits helped keep my spirits up. I decided to call up Sara at Fishbourne HQ. She mentioned to me that several other rowing boats which had departed 35 days before me from La Gomera, were all now using their para-anchors. This was the final confirmation I needed. I made the decision then and there, that I would never be using mine.

I received a message of support from my Swiss friend with whom I had set off a year earlier on the Challenge. He congratulated me on crossing the halfway line and pretended to be gobsmacked by my performance! I replied that I was now in danger of becoming the first person in history to cross the half way line backwards! Few if any solo ocean rowers in history have crossed the halfway line more than once during an East to West Atlantic crossing. I might be about to set the record for crossing it several times on one crossing, especially if the winds and the currents didn't start behaving properly... I also received a lot of support from Owen & Marianne, lovely people. He too had been on the start line with me a year earlier. They could now picture it all from Reno, Nevada. Later in the row, they both gave Sara a lot of reinforcement and advice, ahead of my arrival into St Lucia. Owen was and is one of the greatest ocean rowers of our time.

Here come the Whales

Alongside Atlantic Rower

3 times longer than Atlantic Rower

Whale showing off to the rower

ELEVEN

Pirates

Day 36, morning dawned and I was exhausted. I had rowed on and off for most of the night to ensure I didn't get pushed backwards too far. I felt this was better than being stuck on a para-anchor and going backwards a few miles over the same timeframe. Simon called my performance a fine bit of loitering.

Being a Monday, I just knew I should be able to do better than yesterday. The highlight of my day was seeing another one of these beautiful turquoise fish swimming alongside, then underneath the boat. Given the sea was still calm and the sun getting hotter by the day, I decided this would be a good moment to attempt some underwater photography. For Christmas about 15 years ago, I had been given a GoPro Hero 3 camera. I had only ever used it once or twice, but I had studied the massive instruction manual before I'd left home. I had also invested in a £12 Chinese extension stick for the camera. I figured this could be handy if I was trying to film underneath the boat. I spent the best part of two hours reading that part of the manual again. I wanted to film with the camera attached to the stick the right way up, even though I was inserting it into the sea upside down. If you can even begin to understand what I am trying to write here, then you're better than me. This seemed to work a treat, though I had no way of watching a playback of these videos until

I was back on land. I can now report as I write this book, that all of these underwater films were an enormous success.

I can also now state without an element of doubt that the turquoise fish are not yellow fin tuna. They are mahi-mahi, dorado or dolphin fish as the West Indians like to call them. They are about four foot long and weigh around 10kg when fully grown. They make a wonderful splash when jumping high out of the water, especially when showing off to an ocean rower. The other smaller fish with five or six dark stripes on a light blue body under the boat, looked mighty like pilot fish. This was not a good omen. Pilot fish are carnivores and spend much of their lives hanging around sharks. They swim alongside the sharks, feeding off scraps of food discarded by them. For now, I hadn't seen that elusive shark, but I might have felt him under my boat last Thursday in the middle of the night. Quite frankly, for most of the time, anything could have been happening under my boat.

It was Tuesday morning on my 37th day at sea, I had had only a couple of hours sleep last night and was feeling slightly the worse for wear. I downed breakfast, with a hot Starbucks instant coffee. My thermos mug ensured that even in high seas the contents didn't spill all over me. I used this religiously every morning for coffee and sometimes in the evening for a hot cup of dehydrated soup.

I had been dragged by currents and blown about 12nm south of my rhumb line yesterday. I had managed to row north overnight and was now only about 5nm due south of where I wanted to be. I had rowed just over 35nm and was quite pleased with that progress in these conditions. I had witnessed yet another amazing starry night with shooting stars everywhere. Additional to this light show, I had been blessed again with bioluminescent plankton all around the boat. It is just so beautiful out here.

Last night was one of very few when I wasn't clobbered by waves crashing onto the deck; in fact I was bone dry, most unusual. My Garmin tells me that I have now rowed 1,887 statute miles. No ships around, nobody trying to ram my boat, just one cargo vessel which passed by earlier, about 200m to my port side. By early evening I celebrated, it had been a really good day on the oars especially after what had happened on Sunday. On that day, every possible element had been blowing at me or coming at me or dragging my boat the wrong way. I was now only slightly north of my rhumb line. This made me think that my chances of making land eventually in Brazil or Argentina had significantly faded.

Four different dolphin fish have now been following me for several days. Their colourings are completely phenomenal. Even if I was starving, I could never bring myself to catch one of these guys or girls. On this subject, I had loaded the boat with every possible fishing accessory on the market. I would only use the fishing line if I completely ran out of food and was about to starve to death. If I did catch a fish, the chances were very high that it would get the line tangled around my rudder. I had no plans to jump back into the four-mile deep water unless I really had to.

During the day I had been visited again by a stunning white bird with a single very long white tail and an orange beak. My youngest daughter did the homework for me and texted back that it was probably a white-tailed tropicbird. I was astonished to see anything so beautiful flying around out here. I was still well over 1,300 miles from the nearest land. This white-tailed tropicbird was now doing a couple of laps around the boat most mornings.

My hands are still quite raw, my foot has completely recovered and I'm feeling pretty good. I had pulled something in my right shoulder blade a couple of weeks ago. That small issue had been sorted with another full packet of maximum strength Ibuprofen pills.

Having not heard any news from the BBC or any other news broadcaster for the past 37 days, was just wonderful. Everyone should try this out some time, it's very liberating.

By another complete coincidence it's now day 38 and in the past 24 hours I've rowed exactly 38nm, you couldn't have made this up! My meteorologist has suggested that I only needed one more waypoint to take me all the way from here, to the northern cliffs of St Lucia. I texted 'the Lieutenant' to advise him that I had decided to row past 'Go' and head directly to St Lucia, without stopping on 'Free Parking'. As a result of this, I'm now heading on a course of 14° 10' N, 060° 56' W.

I should just mention here for trainee ocean rowers, it costs quite a lot to rent a rowing seat from that chap in Holland. But if you want to row the Atlantic without getting a sore bum, this is an essential piece of kit. The bog standard seat(s) sold with the boats are seriously uncomfortable. Give this a bit of thought, before you attempt to row more than 3,000 miles. Don't be fooled by anyone who tells you that they damage the runners on the rowing deck, because in my experience they do not. Also give consideration to having your seat fitted with ceramic bearings – unlike the standard steel variety, they don't get rusty and they should last for your entire voyage. They may be more expensive, but in life you get what you pay for.

'The Captain' sent me a text today, suggesting that he expects me to arrive in St Lucia in less than 30 days. I felt this was wishful thinking and asked him to let me know what he'd been smoking. Due to the fact the Trade winds have not developed properly this year; I'm hoping at best to arrive sometime in April. The other thought going through my head today, was that I would soon have to dive overboard again. I could feel the friction under my hull as barnacles and algae grew faster in this warmer water. Having so recently had the encounter with four huge sperm whales, this idea doesn't fill me with excitement.

I texted Sara, explaining that after so many **critical incidents**, my bar was now dry aboard *Atlantic Rower*. What could I do? She swiftly replied, perhaps I could use the cork from the Mermaid Gin bottle as 'an inhaler'… I rowed on into the night.

Day 39, I eventually had a few hours' sleep last night. The only real excitement in the past 24 hours happened while I was snoozing. I became aware of a presence again under the boat; this lasted for a good half an hour. The noise was coming from directly below where I was trying to sleep. It was a sound which I had heard before, a week earlier. Given it was relatively calm, I suspected it must be another very large fish. Judging by the noise, it sounded as though it too was scraping itself backwards, forwards and sideways along my bottom, I mean the bottom of the boat. What this confirmed in my own mind was that I should delay going overboard to clean the hull, for at least another week! Hopefully by then it should have buzzed off. It could have easily been a large hammerhead shark or an oceanic whitetip shark – I knew that they were both common in these waters – but I will never know for sure. I couldn't see anything in the darkness of the night out here and soon I was asleep again.

I thanked Simon for his continuing weather forecasts which were completely surreal in accuracy. I had texted him that I was a happy rower, and he replied, 'You're always happy, it's a good thing'. Light winds were still forecast, around 10 knots from an ENE direction. I decided that I needed to make a slight amendment to my existing waypoint, I entered 14° 10' N, 060° 56' W. If I was able to row this course then I should eventually arrive somewhere between Martinique and St Lucia.

I decided to surprise my eldest brother with a Happy Birthday satellite phone call from the middle of nowhere. It was great speaking to Bro, he sounded very happy on his birthday and so was I. Having a chat and being able to hear all the gossip from France and his side of the family was just brilliant.

I had made a new discovery several weeks ago when I dried off and moved my food rations. I had originally slipped in a 1,000 calorie, scrambled eggs with cheese and caramelised onion breakfast. Today was the day to experiment and try this out for brunch. It turned out to be one of the most unpleasant experiences of my entire trip. If I had been a sensory evaluator (the modern day terminology for a food taster), then my only comment would have been, 'Never again'!

Early afternoon I received a text from Bothways; it read: 'I'm getting excited for you. You are really going to do this. I should have followed you on a very large cruise liner. We could have handed over the Chateau Gloria whenever the cellar was running dry! Keep this up and I'll have to donate again.' Bothways, Talkie and a couple of other very good friends in Australia, London and Monaco had already done more than their bit to ensure the red squirrels wouldn't become extinct anytime soon. Two years earlier, Bothways had travelled halfway around the world, just to inspect *Atlantic Rower*. At the same time, he had begged me not to do it. In fact, I was to discover later that the only reason he had made the trip, was to sabotage the boat! After a long lunch he had changed his mind and became a huge supporter. He could now understand just how small she was, bobbing along out here in the middle of a huge ocean.

By 19.00 hrs, I was exhausted, rowing through lumpy seas with no wind was very hard work, even trying to keep my course was difficult. I decided to call up Sara for a chat and get up to speed with all the news from home. She sounded as wonderful as ever and told me of many new donations made to the Isle of Wight Red Squirrel Trust. This was always very good news.

As I rowed on into the night, I realised that I had now rowed over 2,000 statute miles. This was really exciting as it meant that I should cross the 2,000nm mark in the not-too-distant future. For those who are interested, a nautical mile is slightly longer than a mile. To be precise, a nautical mile is equivalent to 1.1508 statute miles. Just to confuse you further, one nautical mile is equivalent to one minute of latitude and one nautical mile per her hour is one knot.

Friday morning and forty days into the row, the sun is coming up here on the distant easterly horizon at 09.21 hrs. I remember thinking, if I had wound my clock backwards one hour for every 700nm rowed, then the correct time, right here, right now, would have been 06.21 hrs.

The highlight today, was watching the flying fish perform around the boat. With more than 50 fish taking off from the water together, looking a bit like Polaris missiles. Then formation flying for a couple of hundred metres before nose diving back into the sea again.

At 00.31 hrs, my AIS alarm sounded. I could see a cargo ship still about an hour away from my current location, but as per normal aiming straight at me. As she got closer, I picked up the name, Bunun Leader, length 179m and under engine travelling at 11.5 knots. I called up the skipper who told me that they hadn't seen me on their AIS. I thought, well this is normal, and yet I could see them clearly on my system. The Philippine skipper was very kind and they would steer well clear of me. I tried to envisage what cargo this bulk carrier might be transporting from South America to Norway...

At 04.32 hrs, I picked up a very small sailing boat on my AIS system. The boat was called Holly Golightly, she was only 9.75m long and 3m wide. She was a Danish boat, a Nordborg 33 built in 1986. I called up and spoke to the skipper. I had a very poor VHF connection, but I thought he said that they were from Denmark. I just couldn't believe anyone else could be as silly as myself, crossing the Atlantic in such a small vessel. When I spoke to his wife, she must have been thinking the same thing about me. It took me quite a long time to convince her that I wasn't a complete lunatic. They were very friendly and much to my surprise we would meet up again in just over a month's time. It is always exciting to be able to speak to other ships which pass in the night. This was no exception, lovely people called Franz and Mareike.

Since returning to England, I have been able to make contact with them both. They have sent me their original ship's log from that night, during our mid-Atlantic encounter; here is a brief version of their cover note:

'What a joy to get a message from you! Of course, we remember you! It was a highlight of our Atlantic crossing, to meet you in the middle! We were just sorry that we didn't slow our boat down to take a picture of you in daylight. It would make us very proud if you would like to mention us in your book! By the way, you did not wake us up, it was the end of Franz's watch, when after about 8 days at sea, not seeing anything on the ocean, he heard something which was not just noise, but real words from the VHF. He then spotted very small lights on the horizon. As he couldn't see you on our AIS, he thought that you were a big cargo ship, far, far away. Franz was very sorry that he didn't understand the word 'Rower' which is why he thought you were a very special big boat!

When you called again, Mareike was on watch, we were very happy and excited about that contact at sea with you! We watched your lights until they finally disappeared behind us. The crossing from Mindelo to Martinique took us 18 days.'

The Holly Golightly ship's log from that night, read as follows:
'One of those better nights, instead of hissing and creaking, the VHF spark, suddenly sounded *intelligible*, which is unusual. Not because our radio is no good, but because there are no other ships within radio range. Until then (day 8), we had seen absolutely no one – which made the skipper's surprise even greater… But he didn't understand anything at first, the VHF reception still

left something to be desired. At least some small lights can now be seen on the horizon, probably a freighter, the radio officer on duty speculates. About five minutes later our ship's name rang out clearly over the radio and a little conversation between the supposed freighter and us enlightened the night. As fate would have it, we had a changing of the guard shortly afterwards. The skipper Mareike, who is now on duty, is lucky enough to be radioed again by the supposed freighter. As the first female radio officer with a significantly better reputation when it comes to foreign languages, Mareike can bring more light into the dark radio night. As it turned out, the supposed freighter is a 25-foot rowing boat, that is rowed solo across the Atlantic by Simon Howes, an intrepid Englishman. At the time of our meeting, he had already been on the road for an incredible 40 days, having started from Gran Canaria in the Canary Islands. Since he is only travelling at a speed of 1.5 knots, we unfortunately lost sight of him after a while. What we didn't know at that time was that only 32 days later we will see him live again directly after his arrival in St Lucia. Mareike will even have the opportunity to chat a few sentences with him and his family.'

It was still dark as the moon was setting and I could now see Mars and Jupiter very close to it. Star gazing out here was a completely different experience. On those nights with no cloud cover and no light pollution the universe was a sight to behold.

Saturday morning, gosh it's the weekend again and I'm starting to think I could be out here forever. I had mentioned to Simon my brief encounter of a few hours earlier with the nice Danish couple. He reminded me that it was always fun to have a chat with folk in the middle of nowhere. After breakfast, I considered whether I should dive in and give my hull another once over with the ice scraper. I needed to remove the muck which I hadn't been able to get at last time around, plus all the new growth. The water was quite choppy and I decided that it was still a bit too dangerous. The boat could easily land on my head and knock me out. I had had a discussion a couple of days earlier with my youngest daughter, explaining it was a bit soon after my whale encounter to dive back in. She reassured me that despite having witnessed huge sperm whales and possibly sharks around the boat in recent days, in the middle of an ocean they don't just come along and eat people… She went on to say, they only tend to do that if they are near the coast or if they're ill. As we hung up, I thought to myself 'Tell that to the Marines…' I had this vision of one of those huge sperm whales having me for breakfast, just one small mouthful.

The Sargassum weed still floats past the boat on a regular basis. The Sargassum is formed in the Sargasso Sea. This is one of few habitats on earth with no land boundaries, located in the West Atlantic. This seaweed would become a big problem later in my row. For now, I could row through the weed without a problem, although it was beginning to slow me down. Historically, sailors had feared that they would become entangled in the Sargassum and be dragged down into the depths of the ocean. This wasn't about to happen to me…

I battled on throughout the day, the sun was getting hotter and I found myself drinking more water than usual. I enjoyed wild salmon for supper. I decided to give the Barack Obama story a rest and listened to a couple of Agatha Christie short stories. I would be up very early tomorrow getting everything ready for my dive at first light.

Saturday had been a slow day. I spent a good 30 minutes this morning getting everything cleared off the rowing deck. I chucked my rope ladder over the side, with a couple of lead fishing weights attached to the bottom rung, just to hold it in place. The same drill as before, in case I needed to get back aboard in a hurry after spotting fearless sharks. I cleared a few buckets out of the way, stowed my oars and removed the row seat.

I used the hand steering ropes to lock off the rudder, so the boat was now side on to the swell. Attached to the boat for only the second and last time since my departure, I said a prayer and dived overboard. I didn't have to worry about hitting the bottom – it was still at least three miles beneath me! The water was really warm; this was going to be easier than the last time around. No immediate sign of sharks or whales, so I set to scrubbing off more barnacles than you could possibly imagine. Where did these strange creatures come from? They were even attached to my rudder again.

It took me the best part of an hour, probably diving under the boat at least 35 times to ensure that this time it was pristine. I felt better than on my previous dive and had less water up my nose. There were lots of small tropical fish swimming around me, they were enjoying a breakfast of algae and barnacles as they washed off the hull. When I eventually hauled myself back on deck, I felt it was a good job done. The proof in the pudding would become apparent over the coming days. I had already lost about three hours today, preparing and rearranging the boat for this dive. I hoped it might make a difference of possibly half a knot every hour to my average rowing speed. It had only been about 17 days since my first hull cleaning session, but I should be able to get into Rodney Bay marina before it needed to be done again. I poured a bucket of clean water over my head and felt so revitalised that I could have easily then attended a drinks party in Seaview.

I texted my meteorologist, explaining to him that I was now caught up in a very strong eddy current. This was dragging me on a course of 295° – I had been hoping for better overall conditions this week. How about maybe some wind from the east – had he screwed up for the first time since I departed? Simon then cracked a very funny joke. I replied to him suggesting that I was meant to be the crazy one out here.

I rowed on and much later that evening I felt it was time to consult with 'the Captain'. He was still relaxing in a deckchair somewhere in Martinique. I had a long chat with him, but the main reason for my call was to try to ascertain whether I had a problem with my AIS system. He was the only person I had consulted when the boat had gone over twice earlier in the voyage.

Before I discussed my AIS, I explained that during gale force winds, my autohelm alarm kept going off whenever it became disconnected. This was driving me mad; how do I switch it off for the rest of the voyage? I also needed him to explain how to change over the microchip on the back of my chart plotter, without breaking the whole screen. Soon I would need to have the bathymetric map of the Caribbean Sea displayed. As always, 'the Captain' was cool, calm and collected (a bit like 007), none of these issues were a problem. After about 20 minutes speaking on the Sat phone, everything technical to do with the electronics had been sorted. Remember, I'm now going on 68 years old and while this is no excuse, I hadn't got a clue about anything to do with electronics. I still had difficulty switching on my iPhone!

We then went through the different options displayed on the AIS menu, with him explaining their different meanings, while I took notes. When we reached the Targets and Collision avoidance options, I stopped in my tracks when I saw the toggle switch labelled *Silent mode, don't transmit my position.* I gulped and hung up the phone.

Glaring out of my screen I could instantly see that this was turned 'On'. Alongside this entry, there were lots of other options and they too were all turned 'On'. It reminded me of a medical patient questionnaire. For example, have you ever had brain surgery, yellow fever, high blood pressure, cholera, chicken pox, diarrhoea, dengue fever etc. Normally you just tick the 'No' box for each of the ailments, without even thinking twice about it. When I had originally set up my AIS, I had used the same method and just ticked 'Yes' against everything. You simply don't expect a trick question like this one. Every correct answer on this long set up list, needed to be answered with a 'Yes', except for 'Silent mode'. This 'Silent mode' is normally only used if you are being chased by Pirates. In those instances, you can still see them on your AIS system, but they can't see you. In other words, when an AIS transponder is in 'Silent mode', it continues to receive position/target reports from other vessels, but it no longer transmits its own position.

In that split second the penny had finally dropped. I couldn't possibly admit this to 'the Captain', so I had hung up on him. He would have been completely horrified. It was turned 'On', along with all the other options on my chart plotter. I very gently switched it to 'Off' just in case anyone else out here could see what I was doing! This was probably the most embarrassing moment of my entire voyage; it also explained all of my close shaves. From this moment forward, I would never again be compromised by super tankers and other cargo ships trying to ram me. Remember, too, I had set off on my voyage without a radar reflector simply because I never even knew that these were an option. I had travelled the best part of 1,780nm across the Atlantic Ocean and none of these other huge vessels out here had been able to see me. It was a complete miracle that I was still standing.

I called 'the Captain' back, apologised for the bad line and changed the subject. I then thanked him very much for his time and signed off. I would eventually tell him the full story, but only after we met back on land for a good lunch. I had been fantastically inept; I breathed a sigh of relief. 'The Captain' would be promoted immediately to the rank of Commodore. This AIS system information would almost certainly save my life later in the voyage.

I decided to call up 'the Midshipman'. He and his wife had just hit the tarmac on another Caribbean Island for their annual hols. He was explaining to me that his hands had become a bit sore after playing a couple of sets of tennis. How could he possibly be comparing the blisters on his right and left hands, to my blisters! After rowing over 1,780nm, I had almost no feeling left in either of them. Blood poured out every time I removed my thin rowing gloves!

Later that night, around 04.15 hrs, I finally managed to get my boat to turn. I must have broken out of the eddy current which had been dragging me north. I was now heading almost in the right direction again, slightly SW with a tilt to the south. I knew that conditions for rowing would continue to be very difficult for the next few days. It felt good that the distance to the finishing post was only a mere 1,111nm. I now really believed that I was going to get to St Lucia alive, avoiding a lot of embarrassment by making land in Caracas, Venezuela.

TWELVE

The Dolphin Fish

Good morning, this is Monday 27th February, only two more full days until the end of the month. I've just enjoyed another amazing starry night and slightly better wind direction. I'm in a very happy mood today.

The YB tracker attached to the side of my boat had stopped working many hours ago. I discovered that the satellite to which the tracker transmits, may have exploded or have been shot down. Several other sailors involved in yacht races across the ocean had also suffered the same problem of no data. I blamed the Russians for this – I always blame the Russians for most things. I am now rowing against all the odds, backwards at about half a knot. I still have just over 1,107nm to go on a bearing of 265°.

At 14.08 hrs, I dictated a message into my iPhone. I've just been treated to about an hour of real excitement with the wind starting to get up and the waves starting to grow again. After almost ten days going sideways, backwards or nowhere, there is some movement at last…

Much later that evening I could hear my AIS alarm. This was the very first time since my departure that another boat could actually see me on their AIS system. I was in rough seas, and the swell ensured that my little boat was almost completely obscured by the waves. The time was just after midnight. I waited about another 15 minutes and then looked again on my chart plotter. The boat on my screen was called Avantage, she was 87m long. A superyacht, one of the largest in the world and almost spanking brand new. This completely threw me as it was classified as a pleasure boat on my system. It was pointing towards Gibraltar and located a few miles south of my position.

I decided to call the skipper on my radio. He answered and I explained this was *Atlantic Rower* calling; he immediately said, 'We know exactly who you are...' I asked him how on earth could he know who I was or what I was doing out here. He explained that his name was Captain J. Unlike myself, they were fortunate enough to have internet aboard Avantage. He had already spotted me sometime earlier on his radar. He knew that I was trying to row across the Atlantic Ocean alone, and that I was supporting the Isle of Wight Red Squirrel Trust. More than that, he then told me that he also lived on the Isle of Wight! Wait for it... just a stone's throw away from our family home near Ryde. I was stunned, just how cool was this. I explained that I had been at sea now for over 42 days. That my bar had completely run dry, due to so many **critical incidents** and asked if he might consider immediately turning around and dropping me off a bottle of gin. This might just about see me through to St Lucia. He told me that he would need to discuss this request with his First Officer and would call me back. After about ten minutes, my radio crackled back into life. They had concluded a high level board meeting on his bridge. He explained that after giving my request serious consideration, they just felt that they couldn't classify this as 'a mid-Atlantic emergency'! I laughed and laughed; they were now many miles to the east of my position. If they had agreed to come around, the fuel bill for this single bottle of gin would probably have been in excess of US$10,000.00. His boss wouldn't have been very amused. We were all laughing, we had been involved in an extraordinary mid-Atlantic rendezvous.

We agreed to have a lunch together back on the Isle of Wight in the early summer. He assured me that he would be dining out on this story for years to come, and so would I!

As we parted company Avantage continued on her voyage at 12 knots. I started to reflect that if I had been given a bottle of gin, my voyage could have been classified as an 'Assisted crossing' by the Ocean Rowing Society. I had made the decision that my adventure should be completely unassisted and unsupported, and I wasn't planning to change this status now. It was the correct decision to forego a G&T at least for the next few weeks.

I decided I needed some rest and dozed off for several hours as the boat continued to drift backwards. I was soon fast asleep; a nightmare awoke me about an hour later. I was reliving the sound of huge waves crashing onto the roof of the boat from a couple of weeks earlier, a terrifying sound which I would never forget.

I have been rowing for the past couple of hours, early morning here now and another ship called Trustee has just popped up on my chart plotter. This one is 217m long and while this doesn't sound so big, it is in fact over 700 foot long. We are far enough apart and she has just passed me by, doing about 11.8 knots. Nighttime rowing really paid dividends; I was now dreaming that I might make it onto one of those sunny Caribbean beaches before the end of next month. By my reckoning I still have about 1,071nm to go and I've already rowed 2,160 statute miles since setting to sea.

I opened another text from the Red Baron; it was a short one, he just wanted a clarification. I had suggested to him last week that I hoped to make land in St Lucia before the end of March. His message read: 'Is that March this year or March next year!!' I almost died from laughter. I was still a long way from any land mass. Barbados and Antigua were the two nearest islands to my current position. But I had no urge to visit either of them on this outing.

Good morning, world, today is my 45th day rowing the ocean. I'm absolutely ready now to get to the finishing line before the end of March. I've now been at sea for a full 44 days, I haven't seen a soul during this time, haven't heard any news and I'm now quite knackered. I've been regularly suffering from the heat, sleep deprivation and exhaustion. My hands are very painful and eating rubbish food is not very inspiring. I'm also on the lookout for blue marlin. I'm in the zone where historically they have attacked ocean row boats, mistaking them for large tuna. The white hull of a rowing boat, looks very similar to a tuna from underwater. I don't want one of these swords through my hull. If it does happen then at least I'm armed with lots of different sized wooden bungs, so hopefully I should be able to sort it out.

Early afternoon now and I have just had a long chat with my eldest daughter; she and her brilliant husband were on top form, as was our granddaughter. This was inspirational news for me, while I was still caught up in an ocean bereft of wind and trying my best to row in a millpond.

I decided to book an appointment for my return with the local dentist on the Isle of Wight. You can just imagine how this made the receptionists laugh; it's not often they received a telephone call of this nature from the middle of the Atlantic Ocean. In fact, it was so funny, that I also decided to book a table for two, at our favourite restaurant on the Isle of Wight. My incoming call was answered by a machine – you know how they go: press 1 for this and press 2 for that and press 6 if you want a pineapple up your bum. They also stated that while they no longer took bookings by telephone, everyone had to book online, you *could* press 4 if you urgently needed to speak to someone. So I pressed 4. The woman who answered reassured me that I wouldn't be able to book a table on the telephone, I had to go online… I calmly explained that I was desperate for a table for two people at the end of April, but that I had no access to the internet. She then asked, where was I calling from. This was my moment. I'm in my rowing boat halfway across the Atlantic Ocean and I'm still more than 1,000 miles from any land, are you sure you can't take my reservation?!! She dropped the phone, then just couldn't stop laughing and finally confirmed my booking for 25th April at 13.00 hrs. While my satellite call probably cost more than the lunch, it really made me laugh. The end of this story: when eventually Sara and I showed up for the lunch, Pippa gave us the best table in the restaurant!

In between the phone calls I was rowing full steam ahead. By 15.00 hrs it was more than 110° Fahrenheit on the deck. The other news of the day was that I had sighted a total of three Albatross. When you see these guys and girls, you know you're in safe company. One of them had flown right over my head yesterday. I decided to call him Albert; he was to greet me with a daily flypast for the next few weeks. I rowed on into the darkness and by first light there was not even the slightest puff of wind out here; I knew it was going to be a very hot day.

On my 46th day at sea, I've almost completely lost my voice; clearly, I've been talking too much into this handset. The forecast was for some showers and more light winds ESE at around five knots. I have been fighting a northerly current for the past two hours, the sea is iridescent blue and the four turquoise dolphin fish are still guiding me from under the hull. One of them has a bright yellow tail so it was easy to recognise that they were the same fish from a week earlier. My suntan is starting to peel off and the heat is rising. I'm tempted to jump in for a swim, but to save time I will fill a bucket with freshly made water and leave it on the end of the deck to heat up. I'm looking forward to having a hot shower when I throw it in at the end of the day.

The flying fish have been out all night formation flying and Albert has just showed up again for his morning fitness circuit above the boat. I received an early morning text from 'the Lieutenant' who had been busy doing the numbers. In his opinion, once I had reached 959nm to the finish line then this would be exactly two thirds of the ocean rowed. These numbers were marginally different to those of my meteorologist, who felt that 045° W was the exact two-thirds point. I decided that whichever came first would be a good moment to celebrate with my penultimate can of warm Heineken lager. I had only packed six of these, which had clearly been another big mistake. Note to all future ocean rowers: take more booze with you than you can possibly imagine; that way you won't be running dry, like silly me. My exact latitude as I dictate this message is 044° 31' W, so not too far to go now!

I am now surrounded by and rowing through a very large field of Sargassum grass. The area covered is enormous; I find it much harder to row at full speed through this weed. Due to global warming over the past few years, this type of seaweed has multiplied many times over. It gets caught on my rudder and this slows the boat down. The real problem is trying to make fresh water while surrounded by this weed. The first of two Schenker filters is located immediately after the sea water inlet in the hull. This design fault was fine, so long as you could open it and remove the Sargassum. I had forgotten to pack a special tool called a Draper soft grip oil filter strap wrench. Most people have at least one of these in their kitchen, for opening jars. As the filter unit had been overtightened after the last service, I soon realised that it was impossible to open it without this tool. To put this into context, if I tried too hard to open and clear this pre-filter, then the hard plastic piping would have cracked. If that happened, I would be scuppered, I didn't have the spare parts to mend this plastic pipe. I could now only attempt to make fresh water when there was no seaweed around the boat. This problem constantly played on my mind. I knew that without fresh water I would die from dehydration long before I arrived.

After lunch I took some more underwater film of the dolphin fish and others with my GoPro and watched a small black bird trying to land on the nose of *Atlantic Rower* unsuccessfully. This evening after a light supper at 21.15 hrs, I rowed across a large white line painted across the water. I was two-thirds done. There was no signpost, but I was delirious. Maybe I really would arrive in St Lucia before the end of the month; dream on, Simon. After another two hours rowing flat out, I lay down shattered and again felt this very strange vertigo feeling. It passed after less than a minute and I was fast asleep.

Having expected a low mileage day yesterday, in the final event I was completely wrong. I don't wish to start showing off too much, but my track yesterday had been absolutely perfect. My meteorologist suggests I should try to get some south in, especially while the winds are non-existent. With a very gentle NW breeze blowing me the wrong way, I should be able to get further south by nightfall. He also gave me the heads up to check out Venus and Jupiter. They will be very low in the night sky after the sun has gone down this evening.

The following morning, as the sun was rising over the horizon, it's still dark outside at 08.48 hrs, I received a text message from 'the Lieutenant', staying with his brother. He suggested that rowing seemed very similar to sky diving. The only real difference being that sky diving is over very quickly, while rowing an ocean you seem to keep going for two or three months. I had never tried sky diving – for myself the only comparative sport had been downhill skiing. Stepping into the bindings on a pair of 205 Rossignol skis, at the very top of the Olympic run in the Snowy Mountains, then without a care in the world, skiing flat out in a straight line down the mountain. Dangerously out of control, trying to overtake FP on his mammoth 210s. I was never able to catch him and the ski patrol finally banned us from the resort near Mt Kosciuszko. I had experienced the same feeling just a few weeks ago while I was surrounded by 50-foot waves. Taking a one-tonne rowing boat for a surf, with no brakes at all, was really very exhilarating. In all three of these sports, one's life is in the hands of the gods.

I failed to make any water today – too much seaweed around the boat. I figured that I was still about 871nm away from land. All I could do was either try to use my manual water maker (which takes about ten hours to produce a pint...) or just drink a bit less. I have discovered a small bottle of Waitrose lemon concentrate in my rations. I think this is normally used on pancakes. Two drops of this in a glass of briny water is delicious. All future ocean rowers, get a bottle or two for your voyage. It's perfect when your water maker starts to get blocked with the Sargassum; what a taste difference, especially if you've run out of gin.

Later this afternoon I rowed past another oil tanker, Sonangol Kalandula; she was 274m long and 48m wide, travelling at 12.6 knots. I kept well out of her way. I carried on rowing west and have just received a text from 'the Midshipman' at 03.24 hrs. He has very kindly told me that I'm now about 3nm away from crossing the 2,000nm rowed. While this was a major cause for celebration, I was down to my final tin of Heineken and felt I needed to save this one, just in case I was struck down by another major **critical incident**.

Day 49 and my youngest daughter has told me that I was passing over a ridge. While I considered that this must mean a ridge of low pressure, in fact I now understood it meant an underwater ridge. Similar to an underwater mountain and it was creating strange currents. She also explained that she was about to take a four-week holiday in Japan, departing later this morning at 09.00 hrs, from Heathrow. Any chance of us meeting up in St Lucia was not going to be possible. I was very pleased for her, what fun she would have in the land of the rising sun. I rowed on, the heat during the daylight hours was becoming oppressive, 118° Fahrenheit was becoming the normal during the height of the day. It was so calm that the sea resembled a mirror.

I heard from Simon – he and his family are also about to go away on holidays. When I heard this news, initially I completely freaked out. Then he said don't worry about the weather service, it won't be disrupted at all. I wished him a good time, but I didn't want to end up shipwrecked on Devil's Island off the coast of French Guiana. I already felt and looked like a cross between Steve McQueen and Dustin Hoffman in the movie Papillon.

Dive time

Goodnight

Flying fish

*Helping to save the Isle of Wight Red Squirrels from extinction,
Easter Day 2022.*

THIRTEEN

Red wine

A new week begins on my 50th day. I've worked out that the optimum time to make water is just before the sun comes up The fields of Sargassum appear to float on the surface of the water mainly when the sun is shining. I've produced almost 18 litres at first light and my pre-filter looks to be fine for now. I've still got 810.7nm to reach the northern tip of St Lucia. I had a beautiful full moon overnight; this always made rowing much easier than in pitch darkness. I'm now rowing directly west, reminding me of the saying 'Go west, young man' except I'm clearly no longer young. I've been told by my forecaster to expect winds throughout this coming week from the south – this should make life even more difficult for me.

I just want to make an announcement about lunch today. I'm having meatballs with pasta. You may be interested to learn how to cook these in the Tropics. Clearly you can't just turn on the Aga or the built-in gas oven. I've worked out the most effective way to heat them. Simply place the sealed bag with all the contents in the sun on the rowing deck. Turn over after about 45 minutes and they will be perfect. This was a real treat with two drops of concentrated lemon juice in a glass of freshly made water. Of course it would have been significantly better with a good bottle of red wine.

On the subject of red wine at sea, and in case you might think it irresponsible to load a boat with excessive quantities of good Bordeaux, I reminded myself of a story about the great Sir Robin Knox-Johnston. In the 1971 Cape to Rio race, *Ocean Spirit* was skippered by the great man himself. He decided to take along a proper chef and selected a certain Clement Freud. Freud was responsible for provisioning the boat and buying the wine. He ensured there was one bottle per person, per meal, per day... To everyone's surprise, they crossed the finish line in first place, despite the extra weight! You may remember I foolishly set off with only two bottles of Bordeaux for my voyage; this had been another major planning blunder.

It is really, really hot out here now, no breeze and well over 120° Fahrenheit inside the cabin, not ideal conditions for pulling on oars. I settled back and enjoyed my lunch with one of those very large floppy hats on my head. What I really needed now was a deckchair. We had lived in the South of France for almost 27 years before returning to live on the Isle of Wight. The French have a great way with words. A long time ago, the luxury ocean liner SS France sailed the Atlantic Ocean on a regular basis. Their French crew had come up with a new word for the comfortable deckchairs which adorned the main deck. *Transatlantiques*, very appropriate, I felt, for what I was trying to do now, and certainly more comfortable than a rowing seat.

That evening, I sent a text to The Castle Road gang, advising them that I was in real trouble, rowing through treacle. I knew there was absolutely nothing they could do to change the weather, I just wanted to share the problem with friends. I was sorely missing those incredible home cooked Sunday lunches with rare roast beef and roasties. It was to be a very hot and sweaty night with no relief from the heat and no breeze.

By my 51st day at sea, I was starting to wonder if I was becoming unhinged. I've just opened my daily ration bag, and inside is a small piece of paper written over a year earlier, from a dear friend in the South of France. It reads as follows: 'Success is not final; failure is not fatal: it is the courage to continue that counts – Winston Churchill.' It's no wonder we won the war. This was really stirring stuff and whether Churchill said it or not, it reminded me of why I was still out here. I was on a mission and even on the most difficult days at sea I just had to keep fighting on, until eventual victory on a sandy beach somewhere in the Grenadines. Reading these messages of support had become an important part of my daily routine. At the end of this book, I dedicate a chapter to some of the most inspiring small bits of paper. Many of these helped me through the longest days.

As reported earlier, Simon has decided to take his annual family holidays. I felt he was due a well-deserved rest, especially after sending me forecasts for the past 50-odd days. He suggested that the conditions later this week would become 'Diddly squat'! This was really useful information and I thanked him.

I received a message at 13.45 hrs, from my musical sister; it read: Do you get eaten by alligators or savages off Mozambique? I explained that I was actually aiming for Martinique, not Mozambique, somewhere just north of St Lucia and that she needed to buy a new World Atlas immediately.

I reminded myself that due to the excessive heat, I could only charge my Garmin text device after 21.00 hrs. The GPS handset was so intelligent that it shut itself down when being charged in temperatures above 30° Celsius. This was now becoming the normal temperature inside the comms cabin. In fact, it was becoming so darn hot, especially in the afternoons, that I worried my autohelm might melt in the aft cabin. With no ventilation in there, the temperatures where now regularly in excess of 45° Celsius. I made the decision to leave the aft hatch door ajar for a few hours every afternoon. I would have to risk the chance of a rogue wave coming out of nowhere, clobbering the boat and flooding it.

Day 52 was already hotter than yesterday; you might think this would be good for my tan. But I already resembled someone who had spent far too long in the Atacama Desert. I explained to Simon that the seascape out here this morning looked a bit like the movie 'The Day the World Stood Still'. I had rowed north, south, east and a little west, just to avoid the dreaded para-anchor.

Albert came by to say 'Hi' and the dolphin fish were still showing off doing somersaults over my oars. The white-tailed tropicbird showed up a bit later and hovered above *Atlantic Rower*, trying to dump on top of me. I texted Sara, and she mentioned that the Isle of Wight County Press planned to run a story about *Atlantic Rower*. I knew that this could only do good for the charity. I mentioned this publication to 'the Lieutenant', and he replied, 'Nothing yet in Horse & Hound, but will advise'.

I carried on rowing and needed to make another adjustment to the oar height. I was in flat seas; this meant that the oars should be adjusted to be higher in the water. I removed the blue horseshoe spacers in the row gates, then positioned them higher up. This ensured the oars were more or less just off horizontal to the sea. I then decided to call in and speak to my son-in-law, who was enjoying his 35th birthday today.

On my 53rd day in the middle of nowhere, I've got the most amazing sunrise. You know what they say about red sky in the morning, so let's see what happens later today... Simon is convinced that I must be on para-anchor, but I hadn't even thought about it. Winds were expected from the SE at two knots. He suggests I should loiter with intent for a few more days. I took his advice, using this lull to change more of the metal bearings on my rented rowing seat for new ceramics. I then spent some time tidying up around the boat. I needed to be ready in case 'The Big Stuff' returned with a vengeance.

An extraordinary thing happened last night. Just when you think you are alone in the middle of an ocean, right on cue, something really weird happens. I had collapsed from physical exhaustion. My body was shattered after the best part of 14 hours of non-stop rowing, still mainly going the wrong way. It was around 02.20 hrs and I was almost asleep, I had a shooting pain running down through my left shoulder blade. Suddenly from out of nowhere I heard a very strange sound. It was calm outside, still no wind, flat seas and just a glimmer of light from the new moon. The ocean currents were still dragging *Atlantic rower* the wrong way. It took me several minutes to work out where the noise was coming from. I was almost surrounded on one side of the boat by a large herd of whales, in unison they were exhaling through their blow holes. Contrary to popular belief, whales don't blow water out from their blow holes. They blow out air, and this mixed with spray on top of the whale's head creates the fountain effect. It was an eerie experience. To this day I still have no idea what type of whales had taken up residence beside *Atlantic Rower,* but eventually silence returned and I nodded off.

I woke around 05.00 hrs, then carried on trying to row in the right direction. The wind had started to blow gently from the SW. I reckoned that at best I might have rowed forward 1.2nm over the past 24 hours. Simon sent his holiday text message from a local Welsh supermarket. The only one within a 50-mile radius of his cottage with an internet café. I had actually rowed a total of 5nm north yesterday. His mission today was to introduce his new puppy to Welsh streams. This would be easier than risk introducing them to sheep again as had happened yesterday.

Time marches on, I'm still out here on day 54. I've spent a couple of hours trying to gain back some of the ground which has been lost to the southerly wind and the adverse currents overnight. I've managed to get the distance to finish down to 737.3nms from 738.3nm yesterday – what an achievement in 24 hours! I've now been going backwards for many days. Entirely thanks to the massive cyclone located somewhere off Boston.

It's still sucking in the air from the mid–Atlantic and the Trade winds are not blowing. I've worked out that using my current run rate, it will take me another three and a half years to arrive in St Lucia. If all goes to plan, I should make land sometime in October 2026!

This is a good moment to remind anyone else who might be thinking of doing a similar adventure, there are absolutely no bugs out here. I mean you can't catch a bug from anyone else and there is zero chance you might be bitten by a bug. I haven't spotted any mossies, wasps or any other insects for that matter in more than 50 days. I keep being told about the number of people in England with flu, colds or some other bodily affliction. Well, this could be a good moment to get off your bums and try a bit of ocean rowing. You won't be catching anything nasty out here so many miles away from anyone else. With all this fresh air and sunshine, you can't help but feel great.

I've just received another text message from Sara. She has been just amazing running Fishbourne HQ. Coordinating my row, brushing aside any negative vibes from doom-mongers and keeping me up to speed with the fundraising. She now reports that *Atlantic Rower* is featured in today's copy of the County Press. I just couldn't stop laughing – the article starts off by talking about this being an 'Historic voyage'! Almost everything I ever read or hear about these days, seems to be classified as historic. I think that I'm probably the only 'Historic' thing about this ocean crossing! Aside from this, it's a good article and will be good for the charity. It's very kind of them even to bother writing about my exploits. Sara also confirmed to me that my YB tracker is working perfectly again; I still have about 740nm until I get into Rodney Bay.

I am still refusing to deploy the para-anchor, hoping to be one of the first solo ocean rowers in history never to use this nor a drogue. It is now after supper, it's at least 84 hours since I

152

made any progress at all in a westerly direction. This is slightly frustrating. I'm tired of having to regularly turn the boat through 180° just to ensure that it's pointing in the right direction.

It has been a long night, not much sleep and still no progress. The weather outlook was slightly better for later next week. I decided that if I couldn't beat it on my 55th day, then I should join it. I will have another lazy day, doing a few more chores on the boat and contact a few more friends and family. I texted one of my son's godfathers, and we spent about an hour discussing sand pits for new arrivals, for our granddaughter and his youngest son. We didn't waste any time discussing where I was or what I was doing out here. I sent a text to 'the Lieutenant' telling him, for a change, about my progress. By my calculations I had now gone backwards a total of 1.5nm in three and a half days.

As the day came to a close, I had some supper and collapsed for a snooze. About an hour later I was completely surrounded by the whales again. This time they were blowing off in chorus all around the boat. I put my head out of the hatch. I could smell a mixture of rotten Brussels sprouts and farts; I could visibly see the mist coming from several blow holes. This certainly hadn't been mentioned in the brochure. I can't begin to explain just how surreal this felt with the extraordinary sound and the awful smell. They could have been 20m away, but at night in the darkness I couldn't be sure. The boat hadn't been nudged but I was sure these gigantic mammals knew exactly where I was. The noise continued for the best part of 25 minutes, then as quickly as it had started, it finished. I collapsed back into a deep sleep.

On my 56th day it was another scorcher. I carried on and appeared to be going forward at last. Stopping only briefly for food and water, I rowed maybe 16 hours in total. Because of the extreme heat, I continued to leave the aft hatch ajar for several hours each afternoon. It was just boiling inside and I was sure the autohelm would pack up or blow up on me at any moment.

I had hooked up a small disposable desktop fan from Amazon in my sleeping cabin. It was one of my greatest pre-row purchases. They were so cheap; you could almost hear them breaking when being delivered through the letterbox. I had purchased two of them and already one had given up the ghost a month earlier. The fan served to circulate the air in the sleeping cabin, while not being able to reduce the temperature inside. Sleeping was now akin to having a sauna every night, all night.

In between this I called in to Fishbourne HQ to discover that Sara was on top form. She had decided to fly over on 22nd March, to meet me. I wasn't expecting to be anywhere near the outskirts of St Lucia until the end of March so this would give her the opportunity to get some sun, long before she had to fuss about me. She would travel over with a girlfriend and they could have a great break from the English winter gloom.

During the afternoon I was visited by a very large black frigate bird. Initially not having a clue what it was, I became nervous that it could be a giant bat. It literally hung about 40m directly above my head for almost two hours.

I'm now down to my final packet of Ginger Nut biscuits. For me these have been by far and away the best snack food, even better than some of those chocolate bars. Next time you decide you need to row an ocean, don't leave home without them; they are sensational 24/7. The other really useful item which I have used most days since seaweed entered the pre-filter on my Schenker, is a clear plastic bottle called a Life Straw. These are manufactured by a company called Vestergaard. The water being produced by the water maker now tastes a bit briny, due to the rotting seaweed in the filter. This clever straw in a bottle removes this taste completely.

FOURTEEN

Shark attack

Day 57 and my weather forecaster texted to explain the absence of a forecast yesterday. It was due to the fact that the Morrisons Internet Café was always closed on Sundays. He explained that I had smashed it yesterday with just over 44nm rowed. This was such a huge relief; normal service had been resumed.

One of the highlights today was seeing the clear outline of a large ship coming my way, before my AIS alarm could beep at me. She was a cargo ship called Sol do Brazil, she was cruising along doing 15.7 knots and for a change we were not about to collide. She did come close enough for me to be able to wave at the skipper, even though he had been too idle to answer my VHF call.

That afternoon, I called up and spoke to 'the Lieutenant'. He had followed my progress with great interest from the very start, ever since I had told him about the impulsive boat purchase back in 2020. He had been a true friend ever since we first met way back in 1975 and his support for the charity had been unwavering and way beyond generous. He felt that given I was risking my own life out here for the red squirrels, that the king should be told! Initially I wasn't completely sure about this, and we also discussed inviting Sir David Attenborough into the loop. He was another likely supporter for the local charity. He had always been one of my heroes, though the difficulty might be trying to find an address for him.

It was already common knowledge that Buckingham Palace were a major supporter of the species. He suggested to me that this record attempt should also now involve rowing for 'King and Country'... 'The Lieutenant' wrote to SW1A 1AA the following day. I still have no idea as to the content of his letter, but it must have been a good one. A reply was received from Buckingham Palace, posted on the day of my arrival into St Lucia. The reply was private and confidential; I will keep that somewhere safe for the rest of my life, then hand it down to my eldest granddaughter. Suffice to say, risking my own neck to help save this endangered species had all been very worthwhile, just by way of this acknowledgement. After my return to England the charity would eventually receive the sum of donations from friends, family and the British public, for a red squirrel sanctuary on the island. If needed, I would do it all over again. We didn't know then, but later in 2023 the Royal Mint was to announce that the new two pence coin would have the image of a Red Squirrel on one face. While this had absolutely nothing to do with my row, it was confirmation that these amazing animals needed our help to survive and this cause was being supported big time, right from the very top.

After 57 days and nights I'm getting closer to land. I discussed with Simon the difference between the Great Circle (GC) line, being the shortest distance to my destination, and the rhumb line, the constant compass-bearing course. Chart plotters give GC headings. While this was all still a bit of a mystery to me, I was determined not to row straight past St Lucia and miss it!

The Ides of March dawned, often associated with misfortune and doom. I didn't need any of that; my biggest concern had nothing to do with Rome. It was ensuring I didn't get too much seaweed stuck in my water maker filter! I was typically now drinking more than seven litres of water daily. Without any proper booze to supplement this, maybe I was becoming a bit too sensible. I was dreaming of a very large cold beer when I finally stepped onto land. I would ask Sara to try to arrange a *very* cold one for my arrival.

One of the greatest supporters of the charity was a mutual friend of myself and 'the Lieutenant'. He had already given one enormous donation and there was absolutely no reason why he should give any more. 'The Lieutenant' was going to contact him on my behalf with a full update later today. I sent 'the Lieutenant' a text and this was forwarded on. I learnt the following day that the gentleman concerned had very kindly offered to raise some fresh goalposts (something to shoot for), by pledging another substantial sum. This would be paid to the charity if I was able to make it alive to St Lucia. These donations were to make an enormous difference to the overall fundraising. I decided that he was certainly tall enough and deserved to be awarded the rank of 'First Sea Lord'! I would thank him properly when I was back on land.

My food supplies, at least the good stuff, were beginning to run low; I might have to consider food rationing if I didn't make it to land by the end of March. I decided to dismiss this thought right now and ate a couple of Mars Bars to get me fired up.

Day 59 and the dolphin fish are still jumping high out of the water just to show off and remind me they were still with me. I went through my normal routine, washing the salt off the solar panels, removing flying fish from the deck, and opening the aft hatch. Today was the hottest day so far: the mercury topped 124° Fahrenheit in the comms cabin. Between all of this I rowed until I was shattered, then ate enough to give me the energy required for the next session on the oars. I read a message from 'the Midshipman' advising me that I had about 550nm left to go. He had just driven onto the Isle of Wight ferry and he could see that our beach shack was still standing. I replied and thanked him for all of his support. I also had to remind him that this rowing ain't over until the fat lady sings. The most difficult stretch lay ahead of me.

I was enveloped in complete darkness on the rowing deck, time was 06.33 hrs. I was minding my own business and the sea was calm. Suddenly, the transom was hit so hard not only did I get a huge shock, but it caused me to drop both my oars into the water. My navigation lights were still turned off to conserve battery power. I sat still on the rowing seat and within a few seconds the boat was whacked again. I then realised that it couldn't be a marlin – they don't come back for a second helping; it was a shark attack.

Many stories had been circulated of incidents in recent years, mainly off the Strait of Gibraltar and further north, where yachts had been attacked by orcas. These attacks had often resulted in a broken or lost rudder. I still couldn't see in the dark what was clobbering my little boat. I had no idea if the boat had been badly damaged. I was just saying my prayers for it to go away, when it came at me again, smashing into my transom. I was shitting myself. Having rowed this far, to be sunk at this stage of the voyage would be a complete travesty. I didn't have the mind to stand up and look over the back of the boat. I figured if the boat was hit again (which it would be, several more times) then the best place for me was sitting down. It was about 15-20 minutes before complete silence eventually returned. I was sure I must have suffered damage to the transom or the rudder, or both. I had no way of checking either without getting in the water. Right now, in the darkness of the night that wasn't an option. I stopped and had a cup of coffee; it was now about 07.00 hrs and still very dark on the deck. I turned on my navigation lights which were located at the top of the rear mast – still I couldn't see anything. I decided to relax until I could have a proper look at first light.

The sun was rising in the east. I gingerly opened up the aft cabin hatch looking for signs of flooding, water, broken fibreglass or damage to my rudder casing. To my complete surprise everything inside looked to be fine… I came out of the aft cabin and peered over the back of the boat. It was impossible to see what damage had been inflicted without jumping into the water. I wasn't about to do that, given what I had just been through. I decided that as with all my other **critical incidents** to date, I should say nothing to nobody until I was back on land. This would avoid the need to have anyone else worry themselves stupid. Anyway, chances were good that nobody would believe me. I had no evidence yet of this encounter. Once the boat was lifted in the Rodney Bay marina for shipping back to Blighty, then I would have a clearer idea. For now, all I could do was to keep on rowing with one of my spare oars. What an exciting life I'm having out here.

Day 60 and winds are from the east at about ten knots – at least they're now blowing the right way. Clouds forecast today with a chance of showers…that would be nice. I'm going to treat myself to a monster breakfast of wet scrambled eggs with beans and sausages. Later this morning it really rained hard; I just loved having an on-deck shower. It wasn't very long until the sun was out again and the mercury topped 100° Fahrenheit, I was bone dry in no time. I rowed on through the afternoon with music blaring from my Fusion speaker, *Go your own way* by Fleetwood Mac, *Cloud Busting* by Kate Bush and *It's my turn* from Diana Ross, to name but a few.

All three of our children decided that this would be a good moment to mention my row to many of their young friends. The news would go out live today on their social media platforms, Instagram etc. This in turn caused another tidal wave of donations to the charity and lots more interest. I was very excited when I heard about this development – for me another very good reason to pull harder on my oars.

It was a relatively calm afternoon with visits from all the usual culprits, then finishing off just before sunset with a low fly past from Albert. These sunsets were becoming more and more beautiful as I rowed further west. You must realise by now; I'm beginning to talk complete gibberish. This is what happens when you row solo for 60 days without any sign of human life, just the birds and the fish to keep me company.

Around 23.45 hrs, I have just had another close encounter, this time with a ship called Elandra Sea. She was flying the Marshall Islands flag, an oil or a chemical tanker. It's really unbelievable how in the middle of an ocean, there are so many ships out here still trying their best to collide with me. On this occasion my boat appeared on their AIS system and even though I called the skipper for a long chat, they had already taken evasive action. They were heading to Europe with a full load. We were well apart by the time she passed me. I decided to try to have a proper sleep again tonight; if the boat drifted the wrong way, too bad.

TGIF, I started this morning with a rendition of *I don't care anymore*, by Phil Collins, followed by *Walking on sunshine* by Katrina and the Waves and then *The Dam Busters March* by Eric Coates. All played at full volume on the rowing deck. What a great way to start a new day in the middle of an ocean… I polished off a can of Jimmy's iced coffee, which was remarkably cold having been stored in the hull well underneath my water line. I've been informed that I now have less than 490nm to go. My weather forecaster indicates that there will now be regular Atlantic squalls coming my way. I should be sure to fasten tight the hatch doors. Strange things happen in some of these squalls.

I've also come to the conclusion that there are unlikely to be any sharks around my boat right now. The incredible blue fish who have befriended me are now really showing off, they are surfing alongside the boat on the waves. If there had been a white pointer or a hammerhead around, they would have surely buzzed off. I still didn't fancy going swimming – it was too soon since my episode with the battered transom. The boat didn't appear to be leaking, my rudder was performing perfectly. So I really didn't need to be a hero and jump overboard to check on this right now.

I made a couple of major decisions today. 'The Captain' had already been promoted to the rank of Commodore. Today I would promote 'the Lieutenant' to the rank of Captain and 'the Midshipman' to the rank of Lieutenant. These promotions were all very well deserved.

The wave pattern was ideal for rowing, the boat was not being bombed by breaking waves on deck and all was well with the world. It was one of those mornings when I felt like I could move a mountain. As today draws to a close, I calculated that I only have 460nm left to row. If conditions out here behave then it's still possible that I might be walking on land, before the end of the month. Later that evening I realised that I had now rowed more than 3,000 statute miles since my departure.

Day 62 and Simon described yesterday as Fudgy Friday. I'm still rowing my pants off. He is driving back from Wales to sunny Cornwall tomorrow. I may hear nothing for a couple of days at least, until he is ensconced again in the shed at the bottom of his garden. He has been just completely brilliant and very accurate on everything to date. I would like him to be well and truly seated at his desk before I encounter the St Lucia straits, sometime in the next fortnight.

I am positioned only about half a mile south of where I would like to be. Simon has just mentioned for the very first time the expression, *the Final approach* – just how scary is this! Similar to landing a jumbo on the tarmac at Heathrow, you know the drill when the pilot explains we are now on *the Final approach*, strap yourself in, extinguish your cigarettes, place your seats in the upright position and forget breakfast because you've already slept through it!

I continued to row on until I was starving. The sea state had become wilder and waves were crashing on the deck again. I listened to a bit more of my audible recording from Barack Obama – riveting stuff if you ever wanted to be a politician or a president. At the end of the day, I poured a very large bucket of clean water over myself. I even had a go with some shampoo... It wouldn't be long now until I met up with Sara and I didn't want to arrive smelling like a drain. Nightfall and more rowing, followed by a bit of intermittent sleep and then suddenly it was Sunday again. No weather forecast today but the wind was getting up and blowing from the ENE at about 15 knots. This was really exciting compared to all those days without the Trades, ever since passing the Cape Verde Islands.

By day 63 I knew I was heading in the right direction. I had an incoming text from the recently appointed Captain – his brother had forwarded a message from the other side of the world: 'It's a momentous achievement.' This was a real accolade from someone who had already achieved more in sport than most people ever would, long before the age of 30. A quiet morning was followed after lunch by some real excitement at 16.14 hrs. I witnessed my second extraordinary dolphin show... I wasn't able to film them as they were about 25m away from the boat. Dozens of them, leaping up into the air then diving back into the water, just completely spectacular. I decided to commit that moment to memory.

I ate some supper and then carried on into the night. Sara texted to say she was busy making final preparations to fly out to St Lucia. Later that evening I settled down for some more star gazing.

Sunset without The Trade winds

Atlantic rower surrounded by Sargassum

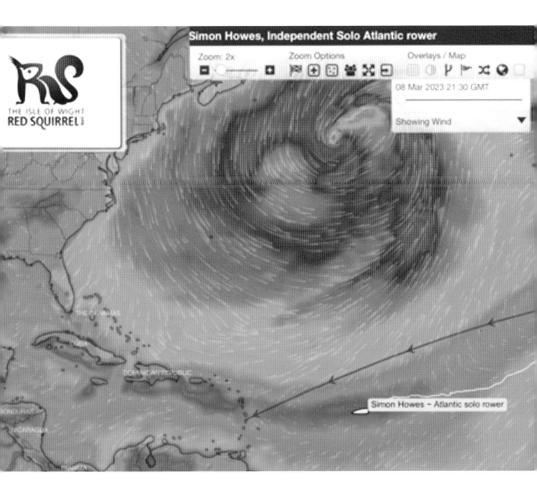

The eye of the storm

165

The Dolphin fish guiding Atlantic Rower

FIFTEEN

The penultimate week at sea

It's really rough here this morning. I was almost knocked out last night by a flying fish. The variety here seem to be different from the earlier species, they are considerably bigger. Three were stone dead on the deck at first light. They were removed by the deck hand (yours truly), before the smell became overpowering. I consumed a bag of nuts for a late breakfast. Talking of nuts, before my departure I'd suspended my standing order for a monthly sack of hazelnuts. The red squirrels in our garden would have to do without while I was at sea. This was having a hugely positive effect on our joint bank account balance.

I carried on; conditions were now excellent for clocking up good mileage. The waves are now large, maybe 25-footers. Still not as big as in the early weeks of my voyage, but big enough to have to stay alert and keep the cabin doors properly closed. It's tricky attempting to use the loo in these conditions, so I'm trying to eat less and avoid having to go!

A little later that afternoon I received a text telling me that the wind would be mainly from the ENE at 20 knots. I've altered my bearing to 280° from around 300° for the reason that I have almost been fully capsized in the past ten minutes. I've decided to err on the side of caution – I want to still be alive and kicking by first light. By 03.07 hrs, I'm only 326nm away from the Straits and getting very excited.

Day 65 and the seas are wild again. As I dictate this, a huge wave has just come over the top of the boat. It is raining properly now and I've had another really wonderful shower on the deck. I won't need to wash the salt off the solar panels today and the deck is looking really clean for the first time in many months. By 16.33 hrs, I have only 299.9nm to be in the zone. I'm now hoping to arrive by Thursday 30th March, unless I have another **critical incident**. I'm running dangerously low on snacks but have sufficient dehydrated food, to get me over the line. I wasn't able to make any drinking water today, so I started to ration myself.

The song *Go West* by the Pet Shop Boys is playing on deck, just to remind me where I'm going. Soon after I recorded this, I had my regular visit from the beautiful white-tailed tropicbird. But this time it was going to be different; she had decided to practise take-offs and landings on the boat... I stopped rowing and stood, looking forward over the bow, grabbed my GoPro movie camera and waited. I didn't have to wait very long; in she came, closer and closer to the forward solar panel which looked just like a runway. Just when she was only a couple of feet in front of me, she aborted her landing. I was then distracted by many more attempts before she finally touched down. This was serious entertainment and up there with Sea Eagle spotting on the Isle of Wight. The final event today was a series of Atlantic squalls – these still seem to come out of nowhere. Very high winds from every direction, a raging sea and with lightning thrown in for good measure. The boat getting tossed around like a child's toy.

Much later that evening I had yet another near collision and it would have been entirely my own fault... The ship was called Mayaro; registered in Japan, her home port was Tokyo. She was bright orange, 175m long and 27.7m wide. Fortunately, the skipper had already spotted me on his AIS. I had been playing various Elton John tracks at full volume on the rowing deck and didn't hear my alarm sounding. I was in high seas with a big swell and I only noticed him at the very last minute. I grabbed the radio and as we talked, he was already turning hard to starboard. I called him back to thank him and couldn't get him off the radio… I even suggested that he might like to make a small donation to the red squirrel charity – still waiting for that one! He was a charming chap; he explained to me just how surprised he was to have encountered such a small boat out here with neither a sail nor an engine. I had dodged another bullet; I had been almost completely hidden in the swell and had been lucky to escape with my life.

Day 66 I had already worked out that this rowing *sequel* was going to be a much longer row than my previous attempt in the Challenge. In any size of row boat, with however many rowers, the rowing distance to St Lucia was at least 140nm further. For a solo independent rower, this voyage is about an extra four full days. Little wonder that only one solo in history had ever successfully rowed this route. It had taken him 116 days, the final fortnight without any food – I take my hat off to him.

In between squalls the temperature today was scorching; my tan didn't have time to peel off before I had another layer of dark brown burnt skin. I had rowed with just swimmers or nothing much else, for most of the voyage. I only ever applied a few drops of suncream to my nose, lips and forehead. This seemed to work fine and meant I didn't have to row with greasy hands.

I wasted some time mentally trying to work out if I could be sure to arrive in St Lucia in broad daylight. Also, I needed to calculate just how many more days this might take. I really didn't fancy trying to negotiate the northern tip of the island in complete darkness. I had asked Simon to make a prediction on this subject. He replied that normally all ocean crossings finish at precisely 02.30 hrs local time!

After lunch I was caught up in my biggest Atlantic squall to date. It was actually very scary, lightning flashes around the boat, 50 knot winds and a wild raging sea. The boat was being battered from every direction and I was completely out of control. Shaken, not stirred, once the waves calmed down, I rowed on into the night.

Day 67, and the really cool news is that I am now only 206.2nm from the tip of the island (note the decimal point). I had instantly worked out that if I was able to row about 40nm a day, then I should arrive early next Wednesday morning. The only problem being that I would have to navigate through the treacherous straits throughout the night ahead of my arrival. Maybe I might be able to slow my progress ahead of this by about 12 hours to ensure a daylight arrival? This thought eventually became wishful thinking.

The time had come to remove the entire electrical board from the wall in the comms cabin. I ejected the *Navionics, West coast of Africa* microchip and inserted a new one for the *Caribbean Sea*. These chips are ridiculously expensive, but they are essential if you need to know with any degree of accuracy your precise position. I would need this data as soon as I was within touching distance of any of the islands. I switched the chart plotter back on again and to my complete surprise it worked first time.

Sara had met up with and spoken to the CEO of the IGY Rodney Bay marina yesterday. Sean was just awesome, on hand to help with anything needed before and during my eventual arrival. He had asked Sara to check with me which was my preferred landing point in Rodney Bay marina. There were two choices: either the floating dry dock or the fuel dock, both inside and quite near the entrance to the marina. I thought about this for about 10 seconds – the floating dock might not be classified as 'Dry land' for the purpose of a completed ocean crossing so it had to be the fuel dock, which was situated on the quayside. Decision made, I continued rowing.

There were no other dramas on the high seas today. I had been warned by 'the Commodore' that once past Pigeon Point, I would be dazzled by all the navigation lights on moored yachts. On *the Final approach* I would be even more dazzled by the neon lights along the shoreline. It would be near impossible, rowing backwards over this final nautical mile to see where I was going in the dark. He had promoted the idea of me dropping my steel sea anchor once I was past Pigeon Point. Then waiting for first light before attempting the final mile into the marina. With still several days of rowing ahead of me, I felt I couldn't make this decision just yet.

Day 68. I had been asleep and was awoken to a noisy chipping sound on the roof of the cabin. I guessed this might be the return of the white-tailed tropicbird. Maybe she had landed again after so many failed attempts on my forward runway. I looked out to discover a very small brown bird. She had taken up residence on the ledge right at the front of the bow. She stayed there until around 10.30 hrs, then she flew back over my head as I was rowing. Carefully, she landed on the edge of my blue bucket and did a poo, directly into the bucket before disappearing. She would be back again, same time, same place tomorrow. I thought this was pretty cool – where do these birds come from?

As I surveyed my rowing deck there was only one very large new arrival which I hadn't spotted during the night. A king size flying fish, even bigger than the biggest I had seen at any point to date during the voyage. It was at least twice the size of a large sardine. My average catch was usually 3-4 per night. Two days ago, the boat had been covered with them. I decided they must have been kamikaze flying fish; they were all as dead as Dodos by first light. This expression refers to a flightless and now extinct bird. In the old days, sailors from Portugal used these birds as live meat for very long voyages at sea… They killed so many of the species that eventually they became extinct. When translated the Portuguese word Duodo means stupid!

There was a fair amount of cloud around and very little current to upset my progress west. I had noticed on my chart plotter that there were two marks on the map in the St Lucia straits. Not having a clue what these were all about, I sent a text to my weatherman. Were these something I could hit and cause the boat to sink? He replied that they were special purpose buoys, likely for some sort of data collection. They had yellow flashing lights on them so they would be hard to miss.

My youngest daughter had warned me to leave my iPhone on airplane mode. Don't even think about turning it on, she said, until I was safe and relaxed in a hotel somewhere. There would be so many messages and emails from the past 70-plus days. It would be better to ignore all of them until I had a Wi-Fi signal. This turned out to be great advice, but it also meant that I couldn't use WhatsApp messaging once I was nearing a land mass. My only means of communication would still be Satellite phone or Garmin text, until I was safely ashore. The newly appointed 'Lieutenant' advised me by text that I had only 200nm to reach Rodney Bay, but I couldn't verify this. He then suggested that this final mileage would be a piece of cake!

It was around this time that EE decided to cut off Sara's mobile connection. This had been our lifeline. St Lucia didn't have a reciprocal provider agreement for incoming satellite calls to a UK mobile. After we worked this out, Sara and I had to rely on sending normal text messages to our eldest daughter in London. She in turn would then forward the same to me, using my satellite text. Just what we didn't need as I rowed nearer to the coastline and imminent danger. In fairness to EE, I discovered later that even the Hilton Hotel was unable to receive incoming global satellite phone calls. The local phone provider in St Lucia had simply not ticked the box for this service.

During the day I was excited to see a flock of maybe 25–30 birds near the boat. It was a clear sign that land couldn't be that far away. I had rowed past the north of Barbados and wondered if they might have flown over from there. If you row the Atlantic from Europe, Barbados is the closest island in the Caribbean, thus the shortest journey time. I had planned everything around going a bit further. I now have just 186nm to go until I reach Upper Saline Point.

Day 69 started in the same manner as yesterday, the small brown bird was back and knocking on my roof with her little beak. I decided to knock back from inside the cabin and this just exacerbated the knocking… It sounded like the noise you might hear when tapping out Morse Code using a paddle. I must be going slightly loopy, we kept knocking back at each other for a good ten minutes; after that I burst into laughter. It's weird how days at sea soon become weeks and the weeks become months, time seems to blend all into one out here.

Our eldest daughter sent me a message: 'I don't know about you but everyone on this side of the pond is getting VERY excited for the arrival of the century. Keep pulling those oars, you are SO close.'

Before my departure, I had heard stories of mariners having problems with Customs and Immigration officials. Particularly if they tried to make land outside of normal office hours. At this stage I had absolutely no idea how the St Lucien authorities would react if I did arrive in the middle of the night. All would be revealed soon.

I also received a text from Simon, advising me not to go 'demob happy' just yet. Did he know something that I didn't know?

'The Captain' sent me news that I had recently overtaken or was overtaking several of the 2022 Challenge row boats. I really felt for these rowers, they had already been out here in the Mighty Atlantic for more than 100 days. I was not in communication with any of them. But I would have surely turned around to assist, had they been suffering from any kind of emergency. I hoped that they would have enough food and make land in Antigua safely soon; they must have all been shattered.

I'm planning to call the YB tracker people on Monday morning. I want to ask them to change my tracker transmission sequence to an hourly signal, instead of every four hours. You needed to have credits with them for this to happen, and I was confident I had enough of those on my account. I felt that this was the least I could do for all the *Atlantic Rower* supporters, especially the Dot watchers. I was to discover once back on dry land, that a huge number of people had been glued to this tracking device around the clock. By this stage in my row, well over 300 people and counting had already donated to the charity. Many more were watching the whole saga unfold. Anyone and everyone who watched one of these trackers was known to be a Dot watcher. I considered this to be quite an appropriate term. Maybe I was going dotty too.

I received a message from Sean in Rodney Bay: 'Hey Simon, hope all is going well, we look forward to welcoming you soon. A big welcome awaits you on such an historic moment.' I thought to myself… So, no pressure then!

On my 70th day at sea the clocks went forward by one hour to mark the start of British Summer Time at 02.00 hrs. In the dark, I have just rowed (surfed) down a wave at 11.8 knots. I think this must be a new record for *Atlantic Rower,* it was an exhilarating experience and just a pity I couldn't have surfed this fast throughout the past 70 days.

I psyched myself up, I needed to pull out all the stops now for the next 60 hours. I wanted to get into Rodney Bay as quickly as possible. I've only got 121.6nm to go, I've also got the benefit of four extra hours as St Lucia is on UTC minus 4. These few extra hours could come in very handy. They reminded me of Phileas Fogg, the fictional gambler in 'Around the world in 80 days', who arrived too late to win his wager at the Reform Club. He had *bet the ranch* that he could circumnavigate the world in 80 days or less. He had been sure that the wager was lost, until his valet Passepartout, spoke to the local vicar. From him they learnt that their journey, through all the different time zones, had gained them one extra day, so he had actually won the bet! They had crossed the International Date Line (IDL), which clearly I had not. *Atlantic Rower* had stayed on UTC all the way across the ocean, I was to gain four hours on my arrival.

I'm still rationing my water, the Sargassum weed is everywhere and no chance to run the water maker. I remembered the poem by Samuel Taylor Coleridge, 'Water, water, everywhere. Not a drop to drink.' I was getting close to land now and had no plans to die of dehydration at this stage of my voyage.

I'm about to consume my last non-waterlogged snack bag, but I still have enough of the dried stuff to get me to the finish. This included one packet of Reindeer stew. I had purchased this before my Challenge attempt, technically I should have eaten this for lunch on Christmas Day 2021. I had also been given a tin of Heinz 'Big soup' Christmas dinner. On the label this claimed to contain Turkey, stuffing, chunky potatoes, Brussels sprouts and even pigs in blankets. It was a 'Special edition' tin, with only 500 produced at that time. I knew they had been selling for a huge premium online, equivalent to ten times the actual cost. I had packed the tin for this second attempt and was only disappointed when I read the 'Best before date', being 02/2022. Congratulations to Mr Heinz for even thinking up this idea.

As I dictate this message there is a huge wave coming at me. It's now crashed on the deck and after a lot of bobbing around, *Atlantic Rower* had cleared the sea water through her gunwales. This was one remarkable boat. I was only 100nm away from the St Lucia straits. Soon after, as if to celebrate this momentous achievement, another gigantic wave crashed on top of me and the boat. I suffered another complete drenching. I'm expecting a NE wind to fire up this evening; this will help my rowing speed throughout the night. I'm so excited that I'm losing my voice as I try to dictate this log.

Almost my last sunset on the Atlantic Ocean

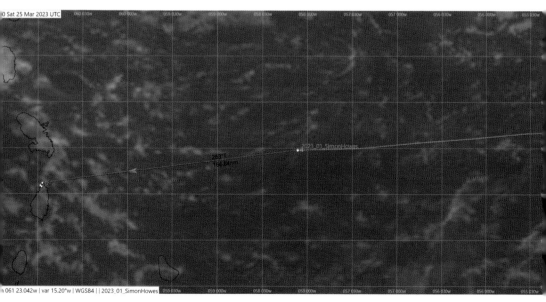

Atlantic rower, spotted from outer space four days prior to arrival

Land Ahoy

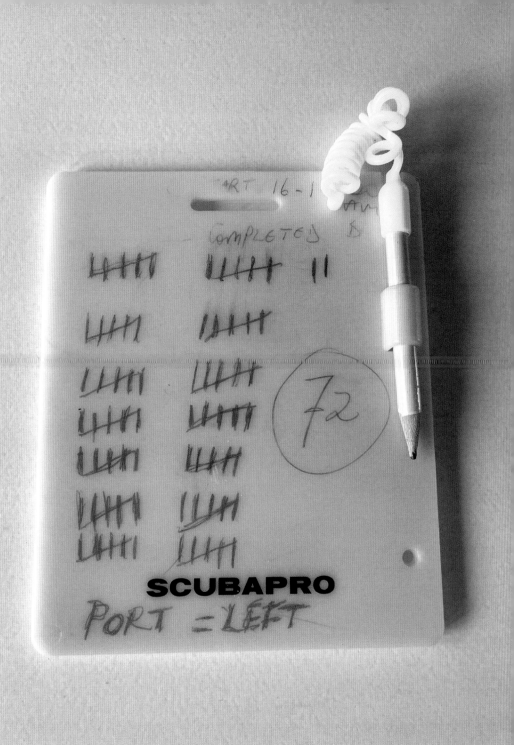

Days rowed – The whiteboard

05.48 Hrs 29.03.2023

SIXTEEN

The Arrival

O nly 74.86nm left to go now, I have slowed down a bit during the night due to a couple of big squalls with lots of rain. Last night over supper I opened a card which had been hidden in one of the ration bags, it was from my youngest daughter. It's a very funny card comparing me to Christopher Columbus who took 70 days to get to The Bahamas, very appropriate for my 70th day at sea.

Slightly less exciting for me… I had calculated that unless I was about to break an Olympic rowing record, I would never get through the St Lucia straits in daylight tomorrow. I would give it a go and see how many miles I could clock up today and overnight. I rowed solidly for long shifts, the sun was still baking me and I was down to my last few drops of water. I was determined not to use or even touch my bottled water reserves. They had already been great ballast. In the true spirit of this crossing, I didn't feel I should drink this. If I had drunk or even used this water, then it could have been classified as an assisted voyage. I decided to try and have one final go with my water maker, just as soon as I was surrounded by clear water and no weed.

For the very first time in almost six weeks absolutely no flying fish landed on the deck last night. I wondered if this might have been because the small brown bird had warned them off. She was still comfortably installed on the ledge above the bow.

If I arrived into Rodney Bay at night time tomorrow, then I could have simply dropped my metal sea anchor and waited it out until first light. However, my sea anchor was located right at the very bottom of the aft compartment. To get that out would be an enormous hassle.

Then, just when you think nothing else can possibly go wrong, it invariably does. I have exactly 54.27nm remaining to reach the fuel dock and dry land. For no obvious reason my autohelm which had performed like a dream ever since I changed it over, suddenly blew up. It was another hot day, but not as hot as some of those days in recent weeks, so it didn't really make sense. Despite the heat in the aft cabin no amount of mechanical genius from me was going to be able to fix this. It was completely jammed solid. I had two options: try the other spare autohelm and hope that it would work, or give up on this altogether and use hand steering ropes. I decided on the first option, but reminded myself that ever since day six of my voyage I had not had the opportunity to test it. In the event it worked perfectly; this was a huge relief for me. Hand steering an ocean rowing boat, through high seas in the dark is not much fun at all. To celebrate I decided to drink my very last tin of Heineken beer. This gave me a massive boost; I had endured another **critical incident** and I felt that this was a well-deserved treat. Later that evening I enjoyed my final ration of Alaskan salmon with all the trimmings and managed to catch an hour's sleep. I wanted to be fresh for *The Final Approach* which would be starting very soon. Just the mention of these words still made me feel quite emotional. A last memory from earlier today: there have been literally hundreds of birds flying around, a clear sign that land is near…

It's now after midnight; the waves have increased in size and a strong current is dragging me south. I'm rowing as hard as I can to ensure I get back on the right track. At the same time ensuring I don't capsize – big waves are now broadsiding the boat. I'm more than two miles south of my rhumb line and just beginning to sweat a little. If the boat is dragged by this current too far south, then I will almost certainly miss the St Lucia straits altogether. I knew that this was the first time in more than 70 days that I could easily shipwreck myself, without trying too hard. Forget sleep now, this was my darkest moment. I rowed all night long until my arms nearly fell off. Come the early hours of the morning I had recovered position from the strong current. *Atlantic Rower* was almost back on my rhumb line, hopefully I had saved her from a certain case of *Goodnight Mississippi*. I was still 36.92nm from the northern tip of the island. There was a fat chance I would be arriving into Rodney Bay before night time!

As I rowed on, for the very first time in the far distance, I could see the lights of St Lucia. This was a big moment for me, I'd seen it before I'd smelt it… There had been a bit of a whiff as I rowed past Barbados several days ago, but not a hint from St Lucia. 'The Commodore' had warned me from Jolly Harbour in Antigua, about the smell of a land mass and civilization. I had replied that I had been blowing my nose on a regular basis, just to ensure my nasal glands were in perfect working order. I was still madly sniffing the air, but to date to no avail.

Simon had already texted to suggest that I should be able to make out the lights of St Lucia sometime during the night. The excitement was palpable out here. For the Dot watchers, I was to discover later that they, too, were now getting really excited. The YB tracker people had switched my transmitter to send a signal once every 60 minutes. Anyone and everyone who might be interested, could be interested together.

It's now almost sunrise, I pulled myself up out of the rowing seat and considered breakfast. The sun was coming up and as I looked over the bow of *Atlantic Rower*, clear as day I could see land and the Gros Piton reaching towards the sky. This was one of the greatest moments of my entire life. I stood bolt upright and just like in those wonderful old black and white movies, clasped my hands around my mouth. In the loudest possible shout that I could muster, I screamed at the top of my voice 'Land Ahoy'… If this had been witnessed by anyone else, I would probably have been sectioned. Maybe I had gone crazy, I hadn't seen a soul (nor a dover sole for that matter) for 71 days, only time would tell if I had really lost it once I was back on dry land.

Day 72 and my final breakfast – at least, I was hoping this would be my final breakfast. I had virtually not slept at all since yesterday morning. They talk about sleep deprivation. I had always considered this to be a nonsense, but I can now confirm it is a real condition. I was now rowing on adrenalin, I needed to just keep going and try to make the St Lucia straits in daylight. But this was never going to happen!

I don't often get very emotional; however, my musical sister has just sent me a text. It read: Mum and Pa are watching and Pa will be telling you to do it just right… I knew then and there that my arrival was going to be emotional. In 1962 my father was the Royal Navy Captain in charge of HMS Devonshire, the first ever guided missile destroyer. He had commanded the warship during her maiden voyage across the Atlantic Ocean. I was sure he would have approved of what I was doing right now, following in his tracks.

It wasn't all over yet. I filled my body with a mixed berry breakfast then set about rowing again. Just when I felt it was almost all over bar the shouting, coming straight at me was one of two gigantic Atlantic squalls. The wind gusts increased around *Atlantic Rower* to at least 60 knots. The boat was thrown around again and again – just as well I wasn't wearing any underpants! Not only that, but the visibility dropped to about 30 feet, as the boat was lashed by enormous waves from every direction. Was this the Atlantic's final test, to try to break me and my boat in half? *Atlantic Rower* by now was part of me. She had withstood conditions way beyond my wildest imagination, this was to be no exception. During the second of these squalls, I remember vividly wondering if my ocean crossing might now end up in Port Stanley. For a good half an hour, with thunder and lightning and torrential rain shattering the calm around the boat, I was expecting to capsize at any moment. This final squall very nearly took me out.

It's just beginning to calm down here now, I managed to get into the aft cabin to reconnect my autohelm. I had been dragged several nautical miles south and would now need to row like a madman, just to get back on course. I discarded my daggerboard into the starboard gunnel – the boat was now listing again on her port side. I imagined that more sea water must have found a way through my Gorilla tape seal. There was nothing that could be done now to correct this. For a brief moment during that final squall, I had become seriously worried that the boat would capsize or be knocked down again.

I stopped for a very quick lunch and drank the last of my fresh water, after all I hoped I wouldn't be needing these jerry cans ever again after today. As I rowed on, the coastline became clearer. In between scattered showers, I was making good progress. Just after lunch when the sun was at its hottest, I had a visit from a bright orange rigid inflatable boat – it looked a bit like the RNLI had come out to greet me. As they came closer, I could see maybe four people aboard and they definitely were not from the RNLI. I wondered if they might have heard, that there was this nutcase heading towards their island in a rowing boat. They circled *Atlantic Rower* but never came closer than about 50m. I wondered whether they could have been Pirates of the Caribbean… I waved, they waved back and then they were gone. This was a good thing as I had no clothes on – my swimmers were hanging out to dry on the grab rail after the latest squall! The nautical miles were really ticking down now, it seemed

I might get to the entrance of the Straits at around 02.00 hrs local time. 'The Commodore' had given me good warning that this would be my most difficult passage. The currents running between St Lucia and Martinique were highly unpredictable. It was really important that as soon as I was close to North Saline Point, I turn very hard to port. Then row like stink to get into the lee of the island. If for any reason I simply couldn't make this turn, then Caracas in Venezuela loomed large.

I felt I should call up Sara to check if the island had just been clobbered by a monsoon. It had indeed, not what you need when you are trying to have a relaxed time by a pool on a sun lounger. I knew or at least hoped that Sara would be at the fuel dock, whenever I was eventually able to row in. What I didn't know was whether any of our three children might also be there. I thought it was highly unlikely that our eldest daughter, having only recently given birth to our first grandchild, could possibly be there. Both she and our son-in-law worked very long hours, either looking after the baby or at work. There was no way either or any of them could have escaped work on a Tuesday or a Wednesday, just to come over to St Lucia from London. Equally, our son was very busy at work. He would have found it nigh on impossible to take a holiday at such short notice. Finally, our youngest daughter was away in Japan until early April. She would definitely not be able to cancel flights and come over for this. It never entered my mind that any of our other close relations might even contemplate a transatlantic trip just to see my arrival. Given all of this, the only thing I was certain of was that my amazing wife would be there. Hopefully with a cold beer, a St Lucia flag for the mast, and bandages. She had now been in St Lucia for almost a week. Enjoying a sort of holiday, with one of our children's favourite godmothers. She had also attended several meetings with Sean and Milton in the marina. They were going to ensure that there were a couple of fenders at hand by the fuel dock, so I could tie up there at any time.

The ENE wind was blowing at about 15 knots and this was helping me row towards the Straits. I had been told by Simon that the wind would drop rapidly once I was on the lee side of the island. Given my current position, that wasn't going to happen any time soon, but most probably in the very early hours of tomorrow morning. I had replied to him that Hurricane Katrina II, had left me shaken but not stirred. I was still afloat after being clobbered twice today; the squalls had now buzzed off. He finished by saying, 'Well done, Simon, keep the land on your left…'

For me, every day throughout my voyage had been as exciting as the previous one. I felt completely connected to *Atlantic Rower* and now I was experiencing the nail-biting prospect of *The Final Approach.*

I had advised the Red Baron that I hoped to make land sometime tomorrow, and he replied: 'What took you so long, I can just imagine all the boring stories we are now going to have to put up with, over the next few years!' Several other friends who had been busy watching the dots, had also added their own sixpences. The truth was, this was never going to be easy in a rowing boat in the darkness of the night. I sent one final message that evening to 'the Commodore'; it read: 'I'll be rowing non-stop tonight, so if I can't call, please don't get the shits'. I didn't need any more pressure, I decided to switch off and maintain radio silence until I was safely on the other side. The only comparable event that I could relate to, was way back on 17th April 1970. Then, Apollo 13 had maintained radio silence during her successful re-entry through the Earth's atmosphere; this was followed by *splashdown.* I was having another Walter Mitty moment, I certainly didn't need another *splashdown!*

Darkness had fallen, the lights on the land were becoming clearer, *Atlantic Rower* was stuck in a current pulling her south. For about an hour I was fairly sure I would completely miss the entrance to the Straits. I had now been awake for almost 48 hours, with less than two hours sleep, so I was getting tired. Then just at that moment a miracle happened. I realised that the current had stopped pulling me south and by a complete fluke, I was now in the St Lucia straits...

I just hoped there would be no other shipping coming at me from the other direction. I was also dangerously close to the northern cliff face of the island. I didn't have a depth sounder and simply didn't have time to look on my chart plotter. I was much too near the cliffs: disaster loomed. I rowed as fast as my body would allow, just to get back out into the middle of the Straits. I remember being surprised that I couldn't see any lights on Martinique – it was clearly a very wide channel between the two islands.

At maybe 02.45 hrs local time, I vaguely remember my chart plotter beeping at me. This meant that I was now very close to the waypoint which I had entered so many weeks earlier. This was the shit or bust moment I'd been waiting for. It was impossible to see in the darkness if I had made it far enough through the Straits, to now turn hard to port. My life was now in the hands of a waypoint which I had entered, so only I was responsible for whatever might happen next. As I pulled hard on my oar, the boat started to turn, slowly at first, pointing in a SW direction. Had I done enough to avoid being smashed up on the northern tip of St Lucia? Had I turned south in time to avoid being taken by the strong currents non-stop to Caracas?

Soon after this I could see lights on what appeared to be a fishing vessel, still some way off, but I was heading in that direction. As I started to row SSW, the winds had dropped suddenly to become a gentle breeze, it was now around 03.00 hrs local time. I paused and called out on Channel 16, is there anyone out there, this is *Atlantic Rower* calling. After a few moments, I was receiving a reply from the skipper of the fishing vessel in broken English. He introduced himself as Captain Charles. He explained that he was out here, in the middle of the night, to speak to me from a safe distance. If I needed any guidance on my final entry into the Rodney Bay marina, then he could shout at me. I felt a sense of relief, I might be able to avoid dropping anchor in the Bay and having to wait until first light. I thanked him and explained that waffling to anyone on a VHF radio, while trying to row solo, was nigh on impossible. I would call him again after I had rowed past Pigeon Point and into Rodney Bay. He agreed this was a good idea – there were a lot of yachts moored up in the bay, all of them great targets for my little row boat…

As we signed off, I turned up the volume on my deck speaker and played *My Way,* by Frank Sinatra for the final time!

The two large rocks out to sea between Pointe du Cap and Pigeon Point are named the Burgot Rocks. These had been used as target practice when British soldiers had been based on Pigeon Island in the 18th century. At around 03.30 hrs local time, I was rowing flat out trying to reach Pigeon Point in complete darkness. I had absolutely no idea that the Burgot Rocks even existed! There are no lights on these large granite igneous rocks, which during daylight hours can be seen as clear as day. It was another miracle that I didn't end my crossing crashing into them in the darkness. It was only after I was on dry land that I fully appreciated how close I had come to certain death and complete humiliation. Luck was clearly on my side that night; I continued rowing and had soon passed Pigeon Point. I turned hard to port to be able to view a multitude of moored vessels in the bay. I could see in the distance the navigation lights leading into the actual IGY Rodney Bay marina. I knew instantly that the great

Admiral George Brydges Rodney wouldn't have had all these obstacles to worry about. He had first showed up here with the Royal Navy in 1762. Like myself, he had been educated at Harrow. He had built the fort on Pigeon Island and unlike myself, would have been well aware of the Burgot Rocks!

I called up the fishing boat and we agreed that he should keep well away from me. Captain Charles would only shout at me directly, if I needed to steer hard to port or starboard before an imminent pile up. I was soon up against the entrance wall to the marina. But it wasn't all over yet. He had disappeared, *Atlantic Rower* was now being pushed by the strong breeze sideways. When I tried to make out the miniscule green and red navigation lights marking the marina entrance, it was impossible to see them. I had not slept for almost 60 hours now and I felt I was hallucinating. I was completely stuffed. All along the shoreline there were lots of green and red shiny neon lights. Clearly advertising shops, Indian restaurants and the like. If the marina entrance lights had been a bit bigger, then it would have been a doddle. I spent the best part of 45 minutes, rowing backwards and forwards along the foreshore. I decided to use my radio again and made contact with Captain Charles on Channel 16. I asked if he could possibly come back out and do some more shouting! He was brilliant, I completed my entry rowing through this very narrow channel into the marina, without pranging the boat.

This may all sound very easy, but it wasn't. With both oars fully extended on *Atlantic Rower,* she is more than 21 foot wide. This channel was so narrow, I couldn't begin to imagine how a superyacht could ever squeeze in here.

Rowing inside the actual marina, I started to hear sounds of people shouting and screaming, the time was around 05.25 hrs local. It was still dark, though the lights around the marina made rowing much easier. I could see clearly now where I was heading, the shouts and cheers were getting louder by the minute.

The first voice I thought I could make out, was that of my younger brother. I had not expected him and my sister-in-law to have come over for this, so maybe I was mistaken. Soon after, I couldn't mistake a voice shouting out 'Great rowing, Papa Noël' – it had to be my youngest daughter... I was certain she was still away in Japan, on a bullet train, eating sushi or okonomiyaki, but it was definitely her voice. Then as I got closer to the dock, Sara, our eldest daughter and our son were all also there, alongside our youngest daughter (how did she manage to get here from Tokyo?). They were all cheering and clapping; this was a great family moment. I simply couldn't believe this was all happening, I was very happy.

Anyone who had been hoping for a good night's sleep aboard their yacht in the IGY Rodney Bay marina that night, was now wide awake. As the cheering became louder, I thought I could now make out the silhouette of Sean and as I was to discover later, Milton his marina manager. High above *Atlantic Rower* was a drone filming my arrival (Sara thinks of everything...) and beside the fuel dock some photographers. Sara had asked them to come along whatever the hour; this was an important moment for St Lucia and for the whole family.

It was now 05.43 hrs and first light, I could clearly see all of my family and my younger brother and sister-in-law, holding up banners, shouting and screaming. It was one of those moments I will never ever forget. I did become quite emotional. I had not seen a soul in more than 72 days; the row was all over. I used my boathook to pull the boat the final yard alongside the quay.

SEVENTEEN

Standing on dry land

Very slowly at first, I attempted to climb up onto the dock and dry land. It was 05.45 hrs local time. To more roars of applause, I stood up on the quayside and had to be steadied by Sara and the children, just to avoid falling over and into the water. As well as the family being on hand to greet me, Sean was also there with Milton. I was overcome with happiness. I was certain that never before in the history of ocean rowing had anyone been so unprepared, so unfit and so unlikely to have succeeded. I had rowed the Atlantic Ocean and was still alive, safe and well. It was a great moment for us all.

Sara had been so efficient; she had even ordered a wheelchair just in case I couldn't walk. In the event this was not required. My eldest daughter had created a very smart banner; the two faces read:

ATLANTIC ROWER, JOB DONE.

ATLANTIC ROWER, 3000 MILES, GRAN CANARIA
TO ST LUCIA.

This was great publicity for the charity. Photographs were being taken on the quayside and in front of the boat for the media. The Isle of Wight Red Squirrel Trust logo at the forefront. This would also be perfect for a press conference, if and when something was planned.

I had rowed 49nm in my final 25 hours and 45 minutes on the water. After the most refreshing cold bottle of Heineken and with the celebrations in full swing, we wandered up the quayside to a local hotel. Sean and Milton had explained they would move the boat into pole position outside the IGY head office. I just couldn't believe how very kind both of them had already been. I don't know many people who would have stayed up for most of the night, to ensure a welcome to St Lucia of this magnitude; it was off the scale.

One of my concerns ever since I set to sea, was founded by other seafarers arriving into foreign ports, outside of office hours. I had hoisted the 'Q' flag, which all visiting boats needed to fly ahead of Customs and Immigration clearance. This was another one of many moments when Sean came into his own. He just needed my passport and the boat papers. This would all be sorted shortly after 09.00 hrs local once the Customs and Immigration office had opened. By 09.30 hrs local I had my passport returned and all the red tape had been sorted. So much easier than flying into Heathrow Airport. Queuing for hours, just to arrive at one of those strange passport machines, which are normally broken.

After one of the most memorable hot showers and proper shaves, it was time for breakfast with the family. There was an outdoor restaurant behind our hotel called 7th Heaven. I sat directly below the name of the restaurant. A rare Filet steak with pommes frites and an egg on top had been ordered. A bottle of good Bordeaux was already being served. I couldn't think of any better way to start the day. We talked for hours, catching up on all the news from home. I then tried to recall some of the most exciting and memorable moments which I had experienced at sea.

During breakfast, I sent the Ocean Rowing Society confirmation that I had made land, at 05.45 local time. They replied, 'Nice, Congratulations'. The man who sent me this reply was himself a complete legend. He had been part of the first team in history to row a two-man boat across the North Pacific Ocean. I was still just a novice.

Later that morning I was able to walk again without needing a steadying arm. I had a message from Sean asking if I wouldn't mind doing a press conference for the local news channels the following day. How could I possibly refuse? Everyone we had already met in St Lucia had been just so friendly. Many of them seemed to think this was an historic moment for the island and naturally they wanted to share in the fun of the adventure. While St Lucia had achieved independence in 1979, it still remained a member of the British Commonwealth. The people treated us, as if we were one of them. I remember thinking at the time and later, that this was one great country.

That evening we had a wonderful family dinner. This was followed by a good ten hours' sleep; it might have been 20 hours but for the press conference at around 10.00 hrs local the following morning. The past 72 days at sea were still very fresh in my mind. I was able to amuse all four television channels who had made the effort to turn out. The St Lucia tourist board were on hand and Sean, who had arranged the whole thing, was at his very best.

During the Q & A, there was a young Danish lady standing at the back of the audience. I had never seen her before in my life. When it was all finished, she came over to introduce herself as Mareike. She had travelled over from Martinique, where their small yacht was moored up. Their boat was called 'Holly Golightly'. How could I possibly forget that mid-Atlantic radio encounter, in the early hours of the morning, on my 40th day at sea? It was very kind of her to take the time and trouble to travel over to St Lucia and a real pleasure to meet her. We really love the Danes. Very few people have the tenacity and courage to even contemplate sailing across an ocean, let alone in a 9.5m yacht. It was great to know that they had arrived safely after their voyage.

I was also introduced to the senior director of The Saint Lucia Tourism Authority; I was most grateful to her for being present. Finally, and to my complete surprise, one of our friends from France, was also on hand for a big hug. Her wonderful husband had sadly died, just prior to my departure. We had been lucky enough to have known both of them and their children for over the past 30 years. They were also great friends with the owners of the best hotel in St Lucia. We booked for dinner that night on the beach at 'The Naked Fisherman'. Helen and Theo were very kind to us and our children, they walked down the 82 steps to the beach, to present us with a chilled bottle of Pol Roger. Little wonder this was Winston Churchill's favourite champagne. We were completely surprised by them and overwhelmed by their welcome. We hope to visit the restaurant again one day, in the not-too-distant future. It is just a great place for a memorable dinner on the beach. In fact, if you are even thinking of a visit to St Lucia, this is right up there with those phenomenal Pitons and not to be missed.

A couple of days later, our family flew back to England to carry on their normal working lives. Sara and I started the process of cleaning up the boat ahead of shipping her back to the boatyard in Essex. We discovered that there was a local food bank of sorts, who would be grateful for any excess food on the boat. We were also able to give them my bottled water from the hold. This had been great ballast, but just extra weight for shipping.

A nice chap from the boatyard in Essex flew in about a week later. He assisted Milton and his local crew of maybe eight fit men, to safely lift *Atlantic Rower* out of the water by hoist. Her hull was then cleaned with a power jet and the damaged vinyl from the shark attack became clearly visible. I can also now report, there were no obvious teeth marks in her rudder. Finally, the boat was craned into a large rusty old container and taken by articulated lorry to the main port of Castries. Several months later, *Atlantic Rower* would be delivered back to the boatyard in Essex, from where I would collect her and drive her home.

For the final week in St Lucia, everywhere we went, our hands were shaken by the locals. They had all seen the news footage on their local TV stations and this was to be our brief moment with almost celebrity status! Restaurants, shops and taxi drivers alike were all very pleased to talk to us, they all wanted to hear some of the stories from the ocean. We were lucky enough to be invited over to meet some of the members of the St Lucia yacht club. Lovely people, they insisted and I agreed, they should have a reciprocal agreement with the RVYC, back on the Isle of Wight. The Commodore handed me their burgee, which I was to present to the Commodore of the RVYC a few weeks later.

We had made one almost fatal mistake. Whenever you go anywhere these days by plane, it's normal to book return flights for both directions of travel, at the same time. Sara had booked her return flight to London Gatwick, when she had booked her outward journey. But my one-way flight home was going to cost more than the full return fare, though there was nothing we could do about that. She had also been told, it would be impossible to get two seats together, on any outbound BA flight for weeks to come. I contacted Simon, and he suggested it might be easier for me to just row back to England – at least that way I wouldn't get jet lag!

In the final event BA were just amazing. Someone had clearly told someone at Hewanorra Airport that they were dealing with an unusual case. One half of this couple had arrived into St Lucia, using a very different form of transport, and he hadn't even seen his wife for more than 72 days. When we eventually departed, I was sitting on Flight BA2158 at least 40m away from Sara. Soon after blast off, a charming air hostess came over and told me that she had found a spare seat, right next to my wife. This level of customer service continued throughout the flight – we were visited by the BA cabin services director and a senior steward with a bottle of chilled champagne. The First Officer then came through to check we were sitting comfortably and enjoying the flight. By this stage everyone else in our cabin was starting to wonder, just who are these people... A few hours later the Senior First Officer stopped by for a long chat and finally just before touch down we had a visit from the Flight Captain. Other passengers in our cabin who had witnessed this, were completely bewildered. Some of them even tried to take selfies with us! This was to be the last moment when we enjoyed near celebrity status.

I had one final Walter Mitty moment as we taxied up to the Gatwick Terminal building. I looked out of the window, just to check if there were literally thousands of people cheering and waving. I was dreaming that they would be lined up on the main carpark roof viewing area. There was no one there!

EIGHTEEN

Back to normal

It was great to be back home again. The St Lucia yacht club burgee now hangs above the bar in the RVYC. I was asked to participate in the Coronation sail past on 8th May 2023, to lead the fleet and to dip my Ensign. Sadly, *Atlantic Rower* was still on a Banana boat somewhere in the Atlantic, so she was unable to perform this duty. A good friend invited us aboard his boat, *Albatross,* to perform the deed. As we cruised past the Commodore and past Commodores, I was able to dip the tattered Ensign, which had crossed the ocean only a few months earlier. The flag was looking considerably worse for wear. It had been battered by gales, storms and raging seas throughout the voyage. Later that afternoon the club Commodore very kindly presented me with a brand new Ensign. I was dumbstruck by this gesture and also very grateful at the same time. Sometime later, I would give an evening talk to members of the club. I would try to compress 72 days at sea into a 30-minute talk – that would require more skill than my row. Many members of the club had given very generous donations to the charity, so giving a talk was the very least I could do to thank them.

A few weeks later, Sara and I were invited to the Sea View Yacht Club to jointly receive the Commodore's trophy. This was another huge surprise. Sara deserved this more than anyone else.

She had been through all the stress of me trying to row an ocean twice and had come through the other side smiling. After the trophy presentation and before a good dinner, we gave a joint speech. Everyone was still laughing when we eventually caught a taxi home later that evening. The support from the SVYC and the locals in Seaview had been staggering.

Despite several invitations, I felt that doing any more interviews for the BBC or others for that matter, would not achieve anything productive, so I declined to sit on their sofa. I would write this book instead.

NINETEEN

Messages of support

Every day as I opened a new ration bag for breakfast, I was to discover that Sara had secretly hidden a card, a note or something similar to make me laugh. These daily messages really helped keep my spirits up, especially after I had run out of spirits! Below are just a few of them, in chronological order. They had been written or composed by various family members and other very good friends:

'Rowing is probably safer than those evening drives home, to La Gorra.'

'The Purpose of our lives is to be happy' – Dalai Lama

'Travel Safe and God Speed' – The Red Baron

'Go west in the open air, go west where the skies are blue, go west, that is what you are going to do, go west, Keep going.'

'I hope that you are doing really, really well and that the waves have been kind to you so far. This is just a little present that I thought you might find comfort in. A St Christopher's pendant. It brings safety and good wishes to travellers, so keep him somewhere safe.'

'You are never too old to set another goal or to dream a new dream' – C.S. Lewis

'Make sure you are properly dressed at dinner time.'

'All our dreams can come true if we have the courage to pursue them' – Walt Disney

'If you're going through hell, keep going' – Winston Churchill
'There will be good and bad days. Tomorrow will be a good day.'

'We trust you will enjoy your solitude whilst we admire your fortitude and applaud you for your attitude. Hang in there.'

'When life seems hard, the courageous do not lie down and accept defeat, instead, they are all the more determined to struggle for a better future' – HM Queen Elizabeth II.

'Every stroke is one stroke closer to the end. Keep it up.'

'The greatest glory in living lies not in never falling, but in rising every time we fall' – Nelson Mandela.

'I thought I would write you a little note just to say Well done. I'm not sure if you will open this on day one, or day one hundred, but either way we are all really proud of you. You are doing an amazing job.'

'Every star could be another planetary system's sun – Amazing.'

'How crazy to think you are reading this in the middle of the Atlantic. Well done on getting so far already. We are all so proud of you. I hope you are singing some Christmas songs today.'

'Do one thing every day that scares you' – The sunscreen song.

'You are amazing! Row, row, row the boat.'

'What a formidable feat. Over halfway across the Atlantic. Alone. We stand in awe.'

'I just HOPE you will not feel you have got to have a go at the Pacific next.'

'You are ruining many a good night's sleep for those of us ashore, so please hurry up and finish.'

'You're getting so close, we'll be waiting for you, Keep going.'

'Eat my rubber' – Clark Griswold.

Then finally, on reaching land in St Lucia an envelope addressed: 'Only to be opened by someone who has rowed the Atlantic Ocean'. This envelope was written by our son's girlfriend at that time, she is now his fiancée, we are really excited for both of them!

TWENTY

The Isle of Wight Red Squirrel Trust – The Woodland Project

I had decided in early 2020 soon after I had purchased the boat, that it would be a good idea to help raise some money for charity. The obvious and easiest way to go, would be to raise money for one or two of the larger UK-based charities. Most of the general public tended to give donations to these great causes, ahead of smaller unknown charities. On a no-names basis, I decided to telephone two very prominent charities. I hoped I could speak to someone in their admin departments, who might be able to give me some guidance on the best way forward with fundraising for them. Bear in mind this was now early summer 2020. The Covid epidemic was now being called a pandemic. No.10 and the media were sending out clear and chilling warnings, that we probably could or might all possibly die. I had read in the newspapers that most of the large UK charities had seen a big drop in income through donations. I was confident my idea to raise some money by rowing the Atlantic would receive a good reception.

In the event I called these two charities a total of three times each, over a period of four weeks. I had explained to them what I planned to do and on every occasion was given the same line. The person I needed to discuss this with, was away from their desk (again) but don't worry they would call me back as soon as possible. Well in the event, neither charity ever returned any of my telephone calls. I did receive a pro forma information pack from one of the two, but this wasn't very helpful. I just wanted to speak to someone, but maybe they felt I was a crackpot or some kind of crank caller. After all, who in their right mind would attempt to row the Atlantic alone over the age of 65, without any assistance? I concluded that maybe a smaller charity might be more receptive to my idea of trying to raise some cash for them.

This was always going to be a no brainer for any charity. Anyone who wished to donate would use a Just Giving link, the cash then went direct to the charity on the same day. To be clear, nobody was ever sponsoring me or my boat. I had saved enough money to fund the entire adventure myself after years of hard work, I was now a retired (unfit) pensioner!

We had been living on the Isle of Wight for four years after returning from a life in France. From the outset we had been enchanted by the red squirrel population, not only in our garden but in many other areas of the Wight. The red squirrels in our garden all have names. Nutkin is married to Nutella, they in turn have six children. In no special order: Nutter, Nutritious, Darken, Rusty, Ruffus and Cyril the Squirrel. Clearly, I had already lost it long before I went rowing! Red squirrels are an endangered species, so I thought that this small charity, the Isle of Wight Red Squirrel Trust, needed my help. At the same time, I acknowledged that it would be a great deal harder to ask people to hand over donations, for a cause which many of them knew nothing or very little about.

My final decision to support them was made on a wet and windy night, while driving home from Cowes, after a huge dinner in the early hours of the morning. I was stopped by the local constabulary. The blue lights of the police van shone very bright behind me, just as I turned into our lane. Before I got out of my car, Sara turned to me and suggested this could be the end of me driving anywhere, ever again!

The conversation with the officer went something like this:

Simon: 'Good evening, officer, how can I help you?'

Officer: 'You are probably wondering why I've pulled you over?'

Simon: Nodding.

Officer: 'At this time of night, anyone out driving who obeys all the road signs, stops correctly at the red traffic lights, indicates correctly every time they turn, etc, normally they've been drinking.'

Simon: 'Officer, you don't understand, you may not have noticed, but all the way down this lane there are signposts stating **Red Squirrels crossing the road, please slow down.** We live down this lane and we always drive very carefully at all times…'

Officer, looking slightly baffled and bemused by my reply, then looks around and can clearly see the Red Squirrel signs in many of the gardens. He then turns to his assistant police officer in the van. She is online checking my car registration, insurance, MOT etc, eventually she gives the senior officer the heads up, everything is in order.

Then before the officer has a chance to say anything else, I was determined to thank him.

Simon: 'Officer, we have just driven back here from Cowes, we have been overtaken several times by people driving very fast and while I have never seen a police officer before in our lane, I am delighted that you are out doing your job at this time of night and wish to thank you.'

At this stage the officer must have decided that given the element of doubt he would give me the benefit of the doubt and asked me to drive on. I would like to pay tribute to all the police officers on this island for doing a great job and for keeping us all safe. I have no idea if I was under or at the legal drink driving limit. However, this encounter with the law was enough for me to decide, then and there, that the red squirrels had to be saved from extinction and that they needed my support.

The following day I telephoned the Chair of the Isle of Wight Red Squirrel Trust, Helen Butler MBE, and suggested to her that I wished to try to raise some support for her charity by rowing the Atlantic Ocean. She was a bit surprised and probably thought this might raise a couple of hundred quid but gave the idea her blessing. I would never have any direct or indirect involvement with the charity itself – any funds raised would go direct to the charity via the Just Giving portal. Helen soon became a huge fan of the adventure and was instrumental in guiding many donors to the Just Giving link.

I decided that corporate sponsors might be a nuisance. They would want me to give talks to employees, after-dinner speeches and have an expectation of ownership of some kind. For that reason, I decided to try to make a difference just by contacting friends and family. I figured that once I was rowing the great British public might also wish to chip in, especially if the media got hold of the story.

In the event, it was the enormous generosity of several Australian friends who helped get the ball well and truly rolling. Years before, while I was working on the trading floor of the Sydney Stock Exchange, I had entered a fun run called 'The Sydney City to Surf'. This was an annual race from the centre of the city, over 14km, through the Eastern suburbs ending up on Bondi beach. I had never been much of a runner but signed up for the run in the late 1970s. I then foolishly agreed to allow the unofficial in-house Sydney Stock Exchange bookie to make a price on my finishing time. When the bell chimed signalling the end of trading ahead of the Sunday race, I did the calculation. If I didn't complete the run in under 60 minutes, I would be financially wiped out. Nothing focusses the mind more than a situation like this. I eventually crossed the finish line in 59m 45s, but I learnt a lesson that day. Never back myself in any sporting event, ever again. Clinically dead, I lived on, to fight another day.

Many Australian and English friends helped inspire other friends, family and more of the great British public to donate to my chosen charity. Everyone loved the red squirrels; they also liked the idea of an old bloke attempting to do something silly, with no sporting background whatsoever. From the outset I had set myself a fixed target to try to raise an amount of £100,000.00 for this great cause – this was eventually achieved in October 2023. The charity has allocated these donations to the Woodland project. On 18th October 2023, after giving a winter talk to club members at the RVYC, I was able to present the Chair of the Trust, Helen Butler MBE, with one of those large charity cheques for this final amount. This had been achieved without any corporate sponsorship. My thanks go out again, to all of those who helped me reach the goal and for your relentless support throughout the whole ordeal. Anybody still wishing to donate to the Isle of Wight Red Squirrel Trust, should now contact the charity direct.

Late breaking news, on the day this book goes to print, I have just received news that the charity has agreed to purchase 12 acres of woodland on the Island, subject to contract. The Isle of Wight Red Squirrel sanctuary will soon be borne. All great stories need a happy ending and for myself this is it!

TWENTY ONE

Summary

M ission accomplished and against all the odds, I had not only made a successful comeback, but I had also made it back alive.

In the process, the records showed that I had become the fastest man in history to row to St Lucia, solo and unassisted from Europe, beating the previous record by more than 43 days.

After my arrival into St Lucia, I learnt that I was now the third oldest person in history to have rowed any ocean on the planet solo and unassisted. I was also the second oldest 'Independent' solo and unassisted rower to row any ocean.

By mistake, I had rowed for more than 40 days at sea covering in excess of 2,000 statute miles whilst completely invisible to other shipping!

I considered I was probably one of very few solo rowers in history, to have ever crossed an ocean without using a para-anchor.

This had been one exciting adventure. I had rowed 2,898.25 nautical miles being 3,335.24 statute miles across the Atlantic Ocean and had survived to tell the story.

The red squirrel charity now had enough cash to buy the land they needed to create a sanctuary.

I have been asked by many friends, what will I do next? My immediate answer to date has always been 'a bit of gardening'. The truth is that I would love to row the Pacific Ocean solo, from California to Sydney. This will require just one major corporate sponsor or a film production company. If you might be interested and wish to have your logo displayed, or cameras switched on throughout this voyage, you can contact me on howessa@aol.com to discuss.

ACKNOWLEDGEMENTS

I can't imagine publishing this accurate record of events, without thanking so many people along the way who made it all possible, so in no special order:

Without the full support of Sara, each of our three children, son-in-law, future daughter in law and our granddaughter, I would never have even contemplated setting out to sea.

My brothers, my musical sister and sisters-in-law, along with all of their extended families and all of Sara's brothers and their extended families. They were all so supportive, showing unwavering enthusiasm throughout the crossing.

Friends of ours and friends of our three children, all of whom got behind the adventure in a big way.

My senior meteorologist, Simon (still the best weather forecaster on the planet).

Sean and Milton at IGY Rodney Bay marina and all of their staff, what a great team.

The Australians, there are too many of you to name here but you have all been amazing.

The Cowes Castle Road gang and the Cowes High Street crew, you know who you are and you make me laugh.

Hubert for his extensive knowledge of local tides.

Jim in North Somerset, thank you.

The Publican and his wife (I hope you may still be available, to star in the Blockbuster movie, more details to follow soon…) and all the staff at the Inn.

The Judge and his wife for arranging a two-day Christmas grotto for very young children, while they dressed up as red squirrels, all for the charity.

Friends around Australia, Bath, Chilworth, Cornwall, Cowes, Crans-Montana, Fayence, Fishbourne, France, Gurnard, Hampshire, Hong Kong, Hyde Park, London, Melbourne, Monte Carlo, Netley Abbey, Newtown Creek, Ningwood, Scotland, Seaview, USA, Villars and Wootton Creek for their unwavering support and enormous generosity to the charity.

All of the Dot watchers.

Duncan, for all of your guidance.

The Fishbourne Newsletter, 5 Stories Isle of Wight news, The IOW County Press, The Island Echo, the television stations in St Lucia and the St Lucia Tourism Authority, all of whom helped raise awareness for the charity.

The great British public and all the supporters of the red squirrel charity.

The Trustees and Chair of the Isle of Wight Red Squirrel Trust who presented me with a globe, outlining my voyage across the Atlantic Ocean.

'The First Sea Lord', 'the Commodore', 'the Captain', 'the Lieutenant' and 'the Midshipman', without all of your guidance, help and generosity, I would probably still be at sea today.

Finally, thank you all from 'the Rower', who promoted himself to the rank of 'Able Seaman', the moment he set foot on land!

ATLANTIC ROWER INVENTORY
16TH JANUARY 2023

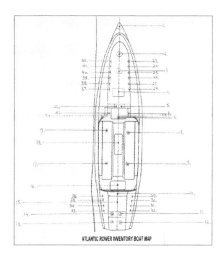

ATLANTIC ROWER INVENTORY BOAT MAP

1 x Four-man life raft (Seago) Box 18

1 x Loo + brush near Box 19

1 x Mirror on Aft mast

4 x Oars (2 brand new) + lanyards

1 x Para-Anchor + 70m rope

1 x 100m retrieval line) Area 15

1 x Rowing footrest between Boxes 17 & 9

1 x Dutch rowing seat on deck

1 x Rowing seat spare Area 15

1 x Rudder between Boxes 12 & 13

1 x Safe up Rope ladder near Box 17

2 x Jerry cans 10L near Boxes 8 & 19

1 x Water maker in comms cabin Area 6

2 x Victron batteries, comms cabin Area 21

Small Loose Items

1 x Back scratcher Net 37

1 x Bailer plastic Net 26

1 x Binoculars Box 4

1 x Box cutter Stanley Box 4

1 x Bungees Box 12

1 x Chopping board

2 x Chopping boards for Jet boil Area 7

1 x Adaptor with 2 USB ports Box 4

1 x Cord (Orange roll) Box 4

1 x Anchor retrieval line Area 10

1 x Anchor (7.2kg)

1 x Rope & chain Area 10

1 x Barge pole Area 15

1 x Blue Backrest cover in comms cabin

1 x Boat transport cover Area 10

3 x Bowls grey (2 collapsible) Area 15

3 x Buckets with lanyards fitted Area 15

1 x Dagger board (with cover) Area 15

2 x Drogues

2 x Fenders (Inflatable) Area 15

1 x Fender foot pump Area 15

1 x Flag pole + RVYC Ensign

4 x Deck knives Box 4

1 x Ear Plugs Net 20

1 x EPIRB on bulkhead near 20

1 x Fishing bag, line, hooks etc. Box 4

1 x Spanish flag & Yellow 'Q' flag Box 4

1 x RVYC Ensign

1 x Fog Horn Net 20

1 x Fusion speaker charger Box 4

1 x Glass cleaner Area 15

1 x Row glove bag Box 4

2 x Glow in the dark pens Net 20

1 x Sun hat wide brim

2 x Sun hats Net 27

1 x Go-Pro extension stick Box 13

1 x iPhone waterproof cover

1 x Washing up cloth Net 37

2 x Light sticks Net 20

1 x 10 Maps (in tube) Between 37 & 42

1 x Mask for Covid Net 20

2 x Mirrors for Distress signal Net 20

120 x Multivitamin tablets Box 21

120 x Puro Labs Vitamin B-12 Box 21

100 x Stugeron (Seasick pills) Box 21

9 x Oar (blue) Collar Spacers Net 20

2 x Oar Grips Box 13

1 x Electronic Odeo Flare Box 21

1 x Pegs (clothes) bag Box 4

1 x Pens assorted, Compass Net 20

2 x Permanent marker pen Net 20

3 x Repeater spare covers Box 13

3 x Repeater covers in situ Aft hatch

1 x Screwdriver (small) Net 20

1 x Silver Tape to block Tri-Light Net 20

5 x Spanners 13mm Net 20

3 x Spectacles for reading Net 20

3 x Sponges On deck

1 x Sunglasses (blue frames) Net 20

1 x Sunglasses Gill (wrap around) Net 20

1 x Sunglasses (Cutler & Gross) Net 20

1 x Torch (headtorch) Net 28

3 x Torch batteries for head torch Net 28

1 x Torch Orange Waterproof Net 28

1 x Torch Black Net 28

1 x Towel Ashdown white & blue Area 15

1 x Towel Green

2 x Travel Towels Net 37

2 x USB cords for iPhone Box 4

1 x VHF Radio

1 x Chart plotter comms cabin

1 x VHF Handheld battery cradle

6 AAA batteries Net 20

1 x VHF Handheld radio

1 x Solid State rechargeable battery Net 20

1 x Water Bottle (Blue) aft Cabin

1 x Whistle Net 20

3 x Whiteboard marker pens Net 20

1 x Windscreen wiper for solar panels

1 x Wood block for Jet boil support Box 17

1 x Wood block for footrest Between 9 & 17

Daily Dry & Wet Meals

Box 17 ~

1/5/9/13/17/21/25/29/33/37

41/45/49/53/57/61/65/69/73/77/

81/85

Box 19 ~

2/6/10/14/18/22/26/30/34/38

42/46/50/54/58/62/66/70/74/78

/82

Box 8 ~

3/7/11/15/19/23/27/31/35/39

43/47/51/55/59/63/67/71/75/79

/83

Box 9 ~

4/8/12/16/20/24/28/32/36/40

44/48/52/56/60/64/68/72/76/80

/84

Daily Snack Packs

Box 8 ~ 1-2/5-6/9-10/13-14/17-18

21-22/25-26/29-30/33-34/37-

38/43-44

47-48/51-52/55-56/59-60/63-

64/67-68

70-72/75-76/79-80/83-84

Box 19 ~ 3-4/7-8/11-12/15-16/19-

20

23-24/27-28/31-32/35-36/39-

40/41-42

45-46/49-50/53-54/57-58/61-

62/65-66

69-70/73-74/77-78/81-82/85

Box 8 ~ 18 x 1.5L Evian ballast

Box 19 ~ 17 x 1.5L Evian ballast

Sundry drinks

Box 8 ~ 6 x Jimmy's iced coffee

Box 19 ~ 6 x Jimmy's iced coffee

1 x Electrolyte powder comms cabin

Box 17 ~ 24 x Fever-Tree tonic water

Box 17 ~ 2 x Mermaid Gin

Box 17 ~ 1 x Chat. Gloria 2015

Box 17 ~ 1 x Le Dome 2015

Box 1 ~ 6 x Heineken tins

Box 8 ~ 640 x Wet wipes

Box 19 ~ 640 x Wet wipes

Food condiments: Area 7

28 x Teabags

1 x Knorr seasoning

1 x Lee & Perrins

1 x Maldon Sea salt

1 x Mayonnaise, Mustard

1 x Pepper & Salt

1 x Tabasco

Utensils: Area 7

3 x Corkscrews

1 x Collapsible jar with lid

2 x Eating bowls

2 x Expedition orange spoons

2 x Garbage bags (rolls)

1 x Metal cup (small)

1 x Metal Fork

2 x Metal Knifes

1 x Measuring jug

1 x Olive Oil

1 x Pyrex glass dish

1 x Scissors

1 x Summit Grey spoon

2 x Tablecloths light blue

1 x Thermos coffee mug

1 x Thermos 750ml

2 x Washing up cloths

2 x Water bottles

1 x Wine glass

1 x Tumbler

Tool Kit contents: Box 22

2 x Adjustable spanners

1 x Allen Keys, Super Glue

1 x Box cutter + spare blades

1 x Drill attachments

1 x Hacksaw

1 x Hammer

1 x Hand Drill

1 x Mole Wrench

1 x Multi-purpose Grease

2 x Pliers

1 x Screwdrivers assorted

1 x Spanners (all sizes)

2 x Spare saw blades

1 x Spirit level

1 x Tape measure

5 x Tie backs various sizes

1 x WD 40 High performance

1 x White plumbing leak tape

1 x Wire stripper

BAG 1 Box 9

2 x Mooring lines

BAG 2 Grab Bag Area 10

32 x Analgesic tablets

6 x Breakable light sticks

1 x CAT C First aid kit

1 x Chocolate bar

21 x Co-Amoxiclav antibiotics

1 x Device charger (NOCO GB40)

2 x Dressings in CAT C kit

2 x Emergency food rations

2 x Emergency water (500ml)

1 x EPIRB (plus aerial)

3 x Glucose sweets

1 x Garmin GPS66i

1 x Insulated Wessex Immersion suit

1 x Smoke floating orange flare

1 x PLB1

3 x Handheld red flares

2 x Rocket red flares

1 x Scissors (in CAT C kit)

3 x Scopaderm patches

60 x Seasickness tablets

1 x Signalling mirror

1 x Signalling torch waterproof

1 x Signalling whistle

2 x Sponges

1 x Strobe flashing light

1 x Sunblock cream

1 x Swiss army knife

1 x Waterproof pouch for iPhone

1 x Waterproof pouch + passport

+ cash, face mask, Mastercard

BAG 3 Flares Area 15

1 x BBQ gloves for fire protection

1 x Laser/LED Flare

2 x Orange Smoke Flares

2 x Red Handheld Flares

2 x Red Rocket / Parachute Flares

6 x White Handheld Flares

4 x White Rocket / Parachute Flares

BAG 4 Carabiners, screws etc. Box 11

1 x Blue and White flexi Rope roll

1 x Flagpole bolts and screws & washers

1 x Various ropes and carabiners

1 x Yellow & Black rope roll

BAG 5 Diving gear Box 11

3 x Barnacle scrapers

3 x 3M Cleaning pads

1 x Face mask

1 x Goggles

2 x 6 Foot harness lines

BAG 6 Main Cabin

Wet & Foul weather clothes

1 x LPX Musto salopettes

1 x LPX Musto smock

1 x Musto blue lightweight raincoat

1 x Offshore Gill blue & yellow jacket

1 x Sou'wester

1 x Val d 'Isère dark blue hat

1 x Wet weather trousers in small bag

BAG 8 Main Cabin

1 x Pillow

BAG 9 Jet boil & Accessories Box 4

2 x Jet boil Cookers

1 x Jet boil new gas cannister (230g)

BAG 9A Jet boil gas cannisters Box 13

4.5 x Spare gas cylinders for Jet boil

BAG 10 Boat Repair Kit Box 11

1 x Assorted wooden bungs

1 x Gorilla tape (large)

1 x Clamp

1 x Duct tape

8 x Tapes various types

1 x Underwater glue gun

2 x Underwater glue (large tubes)

1 x Water bung (black) for deck lockers

Boat Repair Kit contains: Box 11

1 x Araldite twin tubes

1 x Araldite fast-set twin tubes

1 x Chemical glue

3 x Glue spreaders (red)

1 x superglue + 2 x Loctite glue

1 x Sandpaper

1 x Silicone rubber sealant

1 x Underwater epoxy repair adhesive

BAG 11 Seat Covers Main Cabin

1 x Rubber cushion ~ 3 Ply

1 x Spare Dutch seat cover

1 x Sheepskin

1 x Ventisit (thin)

1 x Ventisit (thick)

1 x Ventisit cord

BAG 12 Inboard various items Main cabin

1 x Sleeping bag + 1 x Quechua

BAG 13

1 x Life jacket + gas cylinder Box 12

1 x Manual bilge pump Box 18

1 x Manual water maker Box 2

1 x Harness with PLB1 attached Box 4

BAG 14

1 x Wooden block for footrest Net 30

BAG 15 Box 14

1 x Araldite

1 x Araldite mixer metal lid

BAG 16 Box 2

Tissues

BAG 17 (Clear Plastic) Net 36

1 x Spare deck hatch

4 x Spare deck hatch O rings

1 x Wrench to close deck hatches

BAG 18 Electrical Accessories Main Cabin

32 x AAA batteries

8 x AAA extra power batteries

8 x AA batteries

8 x AA Extra power batteries

1 x Amp & Volt tester spare 9V battery

1 x Amp & Voltmeter tester

1 x Autohelm EV100 hydraulic arm

1 x Autohelm EV100 spare hydraulic arm

1 x Hat with light

4 x CR 2032 batteries

4 x Dominoes blocks

2 x Electric tape

1 x Fuses plastic bag for all electrics

1 x Garmin GPS66i belt clip

1 x Garmin GPS66i USB cable

1 x iPhone pouch with blue iPhone

1 x iPhone spare plastic cover

1 x Jet boil spare

2 x Jet boil spare burners

4 x Matches (boxes) waterproof

2 x S100 remotes + 8 x AAA batteries

1 x Satellite phone old base

1 x Schenker pressure switch 30/60

1 x Schenker relay card 12V

1 x Water salinity tester kit (Code PST)

1 x Screwdriver (small flat)

12 x Small black tiebacks

1 x Solar recharging kit for batteries

1 x SONY Walkman headphones

3 x USB cables

2 x USB Fans

1 x Weather vane + bolts

1 x Wiring wire roll (red & black)

1 x YB Tracker + charging cable

BAG 19 Rowing parts Box 14

1 x Bearing tool to remove bearings

12 x Blue self-locking spare nuts

8 x Spacers, spares for rowing gates

2 x Carabiners (small metal)

16 x Ceramic bearings

2 x Gates, 1 x Plate and 2 bolts

10 x Nylon spacers for Dutch row seat

2 x Oar collars + spare blue spacers

2 x Rowing foot rests

3 x Rowing foot straps

8 x Rowing seat wheels

4 x Rowing seat wheels for Dutch seat

1 x Spare parts for Dutch row seat/bolts.

1 x Steering spares kit and cleats

2 x Tiebacks packets

1 x Wire roll (green)

BAG 20 Sun & Soap Bag Box 2

1 x Dr Bronner's liquid soap

2 x Soap bars

1 x Sun Cream Ultra Sun 50+

2 x Sunscreen Zinc for lips and nose

BAG 21 Schenker Spare parts Box 14

1 x Electric pump spare SM-MOD 30/60

1 x Manual for Schenker water maker

2 x 5 Micron white cartridges 5 inch

1 x SCI Washing product (Code SC1)

1 x SC2 Washing product (Code SC2)

1 x (SC1 + SC2) (Code CK)

BAG 23 Dental Kit Box 4

1 x Amoxicillin (500mg)

1 x Anbesol

1 x Ciprofloxacin course

1 x Corsodyl

10 x Cotton wool buds

1 x Dental Emergency repair kit

1 x Dental Floss picks (pack)

1 x Metroidazole

2 x TePe (medium & thin)

1 x Toothbrush

2 x Toothpaste

1 x Toothbrush electric

BAG 24 Main Medical kit Box 4

30 x Cetirizine dihydrochloride

Aspirin 100 x 75mg tablets

Co-Amoxiclav 30 x 500mg tablets

Esomeprazole 28 x 20mg

Flucloxacillin 56 x 500mg tablets

Ibuprofen 96 x 400mg tablets

Naproxen 56 x 500mg tablets

Paracetamol 152 x 500mg tablets

1 x Lamisil

10 x Blinks for eyes

1 x Crepe bandage

1 x Daktarin powder

2 x Disposable surgical knife

1 x Gauze Swab pack

24 x Gaviscon tablets

3 x Gloves sterile

6 x Imodium Original

24 x Kwells tablets (sea sickness)

28 x Levocetirizine 5mg

MQ Motion sickness patches

1 x Nail brushes

1 x Plasters various sizes

2 x Scissors

16 x Scopaderm seasick patches

100 x Stugeron seasick pills

1 x Sports tape

1 x Sudocrem

1 x Tweezers

BAG 25 Medical items Box 4

1 x Biafine (for burns)

4 x Blister plasters + 1 x Anti-blister stick

1 x Butterfly closure strips

1 x CEL + Rapid to control bleeding

2 x Covid test kits

1 x Cutiderm (Wound dressing)

1 x Ear spray Otomize

1 x Emergency bandage trauma dressing

1 x Eye treatments

3 x Plasters (small)

1 x Surgical Spirit 500ml

1 x Tourniquet

1 x Voltarol gel

BAG 26 Anti Chafe Creams Box 4

Anti-Chafe creams assorted

1 x Nail scissors

Plasters for hands

Shoes

1 x Asics Green Net 39

1 x Asics Blue Net 38

1 x Timberlands Net 38

1 x Flip Flops Net 39

BAG 29 Clothes for Boat – Main Cabin

1 x Atlantic Rower sweatshirt

2 x Musto long sleeves, zips

3 x Swimmers Blue/Turquoise

4 x T-Shirts Gill UV white long sleeve

2 x T-Shirts Gill UV blue long sleeve

4 x T-Shirts cotton

2 x Thermal Gill leggings

2 x Thermal Gill tops

1 x Tracksuit bottoms

1 x Under gardener sweater

BAG 32 Chewing gum Box 4

2mg & 4mg Nicotine gum

BAG 33 20 x Nicotinell patches

BAG 34 Comms cabin Box 21

1 x Rowers Rub

1 x Savlon cream

1 x Soap (Bronner's)

Instruction Manuals in clear folder

Battery monitors (Clipper)

Bilge pump

Padlock combination codes

Clocks in communications cabin

EPIRB new Global Fix

Garmin GPS66i (Full instruction book)

Instruction Manuals for everything

1 x Reading glasses

Jet boil cooker

Para-Anchor

S100 Remote controller

Schenker water maker

Tiller drive auto pilot

VHF Handheld (model HX890)

Paperwork

Boat documentation List + certificates

Boat examination report

Fire Equipment service details

Lifejacket service details (Spinlock)

Navionics Caribbean chip

Insurance certificate

Ownership of boat transfer certificate

R25 Electrical specification

Scan Disc (new) export my data in

Caribbean

Scan Disc instructions

YB Tracker instructions.

Items to carry on plane

1 x Spare rudder block (very expensive!)

1 x Braun razor

2 x Satellite Phones + extras for charging

1 x Fusion Music speaker

1 x Garmin GPSMAP66i + USB cable

1 x iPhone